Bayard: The Good Knight Without Fear And Without Reproach

Christopher Hare

Contents

BAYARD: THE GOOD KNIGHT WITHOUT FEAR AND WITHOUT REPROACH

BY

Christopher Hare

INTRODUCTION

That courtesy title which flies to the mind whenever the name Bayard is mentioned--"The Good Knight without Fear and without Reproach"--is no fancy name bestowed by modern admirers, but was elicited by the hero's merits in his own day and from his own people.

The most valuable chronicle of the Good Knight's life and deeds was written with charming simplicity by a faithful follower, who, in single-hearted devotion to his beloved master's fame, took no thought for himself, but blotted out his own identity, content to remain for all time a nameless shadow--merely the LOYAL SERVITOR. It is from his record that the incidents in the following pages are retold.

The "Loyal Servitor" is now believed from recent research to have been Jacques de Mailles, his intimate friend and companion-at-arms, probably his secretary. He certainly learnt from Bayard himself the story of his early years, which he tells so delightfully, and he writes with the most minute detail about the later events which happened in his presence, and the warlike encounters in which he himself took part; and a most vivid and interesting account he makes of it. In an ancient catalogue of the Mazarine Library, his book is first set down as the ***Histoire du Chevalier Bayard, par*** Jacques de Mailles, Paris, in 4to, 1514 (probably a mistake for 1524). The better-known edition, with only the name of the "Loyal Servitor," was published in 1527, under the title of

THE VERY JOYFUL AND VERY DELIGHTFUL
HISTORY
OF THE LIFE, THE HEROIC DEEDS, THE TRIUMPHS
AND THE VALOUR OF THE GOOD KNIGHT
WITHOUT FEAR AND WITHOUT REPROACH

CHAPTER I

Pierre Terrail, the renowned Bayard of history, was born at the Castle of Bayard, in Dauphine, about the year 1474, when Louis XI. was King of France. He came of an ancient and heroic race, whose chief privilege had been to shed their blood for France throughout the Middle Ages.

The lord of Bayard had married Helene Alleman, a good and pious lady of a noble family, whose brother Laurent was the Bishop of Grenoble. Pierre Bayard, the hero of this story, was the second son of a large family; he had three brothers and four sisters. His eldest brother, Georges, was five or six years older than himself, then came his sisters, Catherine, Jeanne, and Marie, while younger than himself were Claudie, and two brothers, Jacques and Philippe.

Like so many other mediaeval strongholds, the Castle of Bayard was built upon a rocky hill, which always gave an advantage in case of attack. It had been erected by the great-grandfather and namesake of our Pierre Bayard, probably on the site of an earlier stronghold, in the year 1404. No better position could have been chosen, for it commanded a deep valley on two sides, in a wild and mountainous district of Dauphine, near the village of Pontcharra in the Graisivaudan. Even now we can still see from its ruins what a powerful fortress it was in its time, with massive towers three stories high, standing out well in front of the castle wall, and defended by a strong drawbridge. Well fortified, it could have stood a siege before the days of artillery.

But towards the end of the fifteenth century, when Bayard's childhood was spent here, such castles as these were not looked upon as mainly places of defence and refuge, they were gradually becoming more like the later manor-houses--family homes, with comfortable chambers and halls, where once there had chiefly been the rude dwelling of a garrison used for defence and stored with missiles and arms.

Each story of the castle, as well as the towers, would contain various chambers, well lighted with windows pierced in the thick stone walls. On the first floor, approached by a broad flight of steps from the court, we find the oratory--scarcely large enough to be dignified by the name of chapel--the dining-hall, and the private chamber of the lord of the castle. On the floor above this the lady of Bayard had her own apartment, the "garde-robe" or closet where her dresses were kept, and the place where her daughters as they grew up, and any maidens who were brought up under her care, sat at their needlework, and where they slept at night. On the upper story were the rooms for the young children with their maids, and the various guest-chambers.

The ground floor below the dining-halls was a dark place given up to storerooms and the servants' quarters, and below this again were cellars and grim dungeons, which could only be reached by trap-doors. The kitchen, usually a round building, stood in an outer court, and here great wood fires could be used for the needful hospitality of a country house. The stables and the rough quarters for the serving-men were beyond.

The dining-hall was used as a court of justice when the lord of the castle had to settle any difficulties, to receive his dues, or reprimand and punish any refractory vassal. At one end of this hall was a great hearth, where most substantial logs of wood could be laid across the fire-dogs, and burn with a cheerful blaze to light and warm the company in the long, cold winter evenings. At meal-times trestle tables were brought in, and on these the food was served, the long benches being placed on each side of them. On the special occasions of important visits or unusual festivities, a high table was set out at the upper end. The floor was covered with fresh rushes, skins of wolf or bear being laid before the fire, and the walls were stencilled in white and yellow on the higher part, and hung with serge or frieze below. Only in the lady's chamber do we find carpets and hangings of tapestry or embroidery, part of her wedding dowry or the work of her maidens. Here, too, were a few soft cushions on the floor to sit upon, some carved chairs, tables, and coffers. The master of the house always had his great arm-chair with a head, and curtains to keep off the draughts, which were many and bitterly cold in winter-time.

The chronicler of Bayard, known as the "Loyal Servitor," begins his story on a spring day of the year 1487.

Aymon Terrail, lord of Bayard, sat by the fireside in his own chamber, the walls of which were hung with old arms and trophies of the chase. He felt ill and out of spirits. He was growing old--he had not long to live: so he assured his good wife.

What was to become of his sons when he was gone? A sudden thought occurred to him. "I will send for them at once, and we will give them a voice in the matter."

To this the lady of Bayard agreed, for she never crossed her lord's will, and at least it would distract his gloomy thoughts. It chanced that all the four lads were at home, and ready to obey their father's command. As they entered the room and came forward, one by one, in front of the great chair by the hearth, somewhat awed by this hasty summons, they were encouraged by a smile from their mother, who sat quietly in the background with her embroidery.

The assembled group made a striking picture. The grand old man, a massive figure seated in his canopied arm-chair, with white hair and flowing beard and piercing black eyes, was closely wrapped in a long dark robe lined with fur, and wore a velvet cap which came down over his shaggy brows. Before him stood his four well-grown, sturdy, ruddy-faced boys, awaiting his pleasure with seemly reverence, for none of them would have dared to be seated unbidden in the presence of their father. Aymon de Bayard turned to his eldest son, a big, strongly-built youth of eighteen, and asked him what career in life he would like to follow. Georges, who knew that he was heir to the domain and that he would probably not have long to wait for his succession, made answer respectfully that he never wished to leave his home, and that he would serve his father faithfully to the end of his days. Possibly this was what the lord of Bayard expected, for he showed no surprise, but simply replied, "Very well, Georges, as you love your home you shall stay here and go a-hunting to fight the bears."

Next in order came Pierre, the "Good Knight" of history, who was then thirteen years of age, as lively as a cricket, and who replied with a smiling face, "My lord and father, although my love for you would keep me in your service, yet you have so rooted in my heart the story of noble men of the past, especially of our house, that if it please you, I will follow the profession of arms like you and your ancestors. It is that which I desire more than anything else in the world, and I trust that by the help of God's grace I may not dishonour you."

The third son, Jacques, said that he wished to follow in the steps of his uncle, Monseigneur d'Ainay, the prior of a rich abbey near Lyons. The youngest boy, Philippe, made the same choice, and said that he would wish to be like his uncle, the Bishop of Grenoble.

After this conversation with his four sons the lord of Bayard, not being able to ride forth himself, sent one of his servants on the morrow to Grenoble, about eighteen miles distant, with a letter to his brother-in-law the Bishop, begging him to come to his Castle of Bayard as he had important things to say to him. The good Bishop, who was always delighted to give pleasure to any one, readily agreed. He set off as soon as he had received the letter, and arrived in due time at the castle, where he found Aymon de Bayard seated in his great chair by the fire. They greeted each other warmly and spent a very pleasant evening together with several other gentlemen of Dauphine, guests of the house.

At the end of dinner, the venerable lord of Bayard thus addressed the company: "My lord Bishop, and you, my lords, it is time to tell you the reason for which I have called you together. You see that I am so oppressed with age that it is hardly possible I can live two years. God has given me four sons, each of whom has told me what he would like to do. My son Pierre told me that he would follow the calling of arms, and thus gave me singular pleasure. He greatly resembles my late father, and if he is like him in his deeds he cannot fail to be a great and noble knight. It is needful for his training that I should place him in the household of some prince or lord where he may learn aright his profession. I pray you that you will each tell me what great House you advise."

Then said one of the ancient knights: "He must be sent to the King of France." Another suggested that he would do very well with the Duke of Bourbon; and thus one after another gave his advice. At last the Bishop of Grenoble spoke: "My brother, you know that we are in great friendship with the Duke Charles of Savoy, and that he holds us in the number of his faithful vassals. I think that he would willingly take the boy as one of his pages. He is at Chambery, which is near here; and if it seems good to you, and to the company, I will take him there to-morrow morning."

This proposal of the Bishop of Grenoble seemed excellent to all present, and Pierre Bayard was formally presented to him by his father, who said: "Take him, my lord, and may God grant that he prove a worthy gift and do you honour by his life." The Bishop at once sent in haste to Grenoble with orders to his own tailor to bring velvet, satin, and all things needful to make a noble page presentable. It was a night to be long remembered in the castle, for cunning hands were pressed into the service under the eyes of the master tailor, who stitched away through the long hours in such style that next morning all was ready. A proud and happy boy was Bayard the next morning when, after breakfast, clad in his fine new clothes, he rode the chestnut horse into the courtyard before the admiring gaze, of all the company assembled to look upon him.

When the spirited animal felt that he had such a light weight upon his back, while at the same time he was urged on with spurs, he began to prance about in the most lively fashion, and everybody expected to see the boy thrown off. But Bayard kept his seat like a man of thirty, spurred on his horse, and galloped round and round the court, as brave as a lion, his eyes sparkling with delight. An old soldier like his father thoroughly appreciated the lad's nerve and spirit, and could scarcely help betraying the pride he felt in him. But the wise Bishop probably thought that the lad had received quite as much notice as was good for him, and announced that he was ready to start, adding to his nephew: "Now, my friend, you had better not dismount, but take leave of all the company."

Bayard first turned to his father with a beaming countenance. "My lord and father, I pray God that He may give you a good and long life, and trust that before you are taken from this world you may have good news of me." "My son, such is my prayer," was the old man's reply as he gave the boy his blessing. Bayard then took leave of all the gentlemen present, one after the other. Meantime the poor lady his mother was in her tower chamber, where she was busy to the last moment packing a little chest with such things as she knew her boy would need in his new life. Although she was glad of the fair prospect before him, and very proud of her son, yet she could not restrain her tears at the thought of parting from him; for such is the way of mothers.

Yet when they came and told her, "Madame, if you would like to see your son he is on horseback all ready to start," the good lady went bravely down to the little postern door behind the tower and sent for Pierre to come to her. As the boy rode up proudly at her summons and bending low in his saddle took off his plumed cap in smiling salutation, he was a gallant sight for loving eyes to rest upon. Bayard never forgot his mother's parting words. "Pierre, my boy, you are going into the service of a noble prince. In so far as a mother can rule her child, I command you three things, and if you do them, be assured that you will live triumphantly in this world. The first is that above all things you should ever fear and serve God; seek His help night and morning and He will help you. The second is that you should be gentle and courteous to all men, being yourself free from all pride. Be ever humble and helpful, avoiding envy, flattery, and tale-bearing. Be loyal, my son, in word and deed, that all men may have perfect trust in you. Thirdly, with the goods that God may give you, be ever full of charity to the poor, and freely generous to all men. And may God give us grace that while we live we may always hear you well spoken of."

In a few simple words the boy promised to remember, and took a loving farewell of her. Then his lady mother drew from her sleeve a little purse, in which were her private savings: six gold crowns and one in small change,[1] and this she gave to her son. Also, calling one of the attendants of the Bishop, she entrusted him with the little trunk containing linen and other necessaries for Bayard, begging him to give it in the care of the equerry who would have charge of the boy at the Duke of Savoy's Court, and she gave him two crowns. There was no time for more, as the Bishop of Grenoble was now calling his nephew. As he set forth on that Saturday morning, riding his spirited chestnut towards Chambery, with the sun shining and the birds singing, and all his future like a fair vision before him, young Bayard thought that he was in paradise.

Pierre Bayard had set forth from his home in the early morning, soon after breakfast, and he rode all day by the side of his uncle until, in the evening, they reached the town of Chambery, where all the clergy came out to meet the Bishop of Grenoble, for this was part of his diocese, where he had his official dwelling. That night he remained at his lodging without showing himself at Court, although the Duke was soon informed of his arrival, at which he was very pleased. The next morning, which was Sunday, the Bishop rose very early and went to pay his respects to the Duke of Savoy, who received him with the greatest favour, and had a long talk with him all the way from the castle to the church, where the Bishop of Grenoble said Mass with great ceremony. When this was over, the Duke led him

1   The gold crown was then worth 1 livre 15 sous. Multiplying this by 31, in order to find its present value, we learn that the sum which Bayard received from his mother would to-day be worth 266 francs, or about 10 guineas.

by the hand to dine with him, and at this meal young Bayard waited upon his uncle and poured out his wine with much skill and care. The Duke noticed this youthful cup-bearer and asked the Bishop, "My lord of Grenoble, who is this young boy who is serving you?"

"My lord," was the reply, "this is a man-at-arms whom I have come to present to you for your service if you will be pleased to accept him. But he is not now in the condition in which I desire to give him to you; after dinner, if it is your pleasure, you will see him."

"It would be very strange if I refused such a present," said the Duke, who had already taken a fancy to the boy.

Now young Bayard, who had already received instructions from his uncle, wasted no time over his own dinner, but hurried back to get his horse saddled and in good order, then he rode quietly into the courtyard of the castle. The Duke of Savoy was, as usual, resting after dinner in the long gallery, or **perron**, built the whole length of the keep, on a level with the first floor, and overlooking the great courtyard below. It was like a cloister, with great arched windows, and served for a general meeting-place or lounge in cold or wet weather. From thence he could see the boy going through all his pretty feats of horsemanship as if he had been a man of thirty who had been trained to war all his life. He was greatly pleased, and turning to the Bishop of Grenoble he said to him, "My lord, I believe that is your little favourite who is riding so well?"

"You are quite right, my lord Duke," was the answer. "He is my nephew, and comes of a race where there have been many gallant knights. His father, who from the wounds he has received in battle, and from advancing age, is unable to come himself to your Court, recommends himself very humbly to your good grace, and makes you a present of the boy."

"By my faith!" exclaimed the Duke, "I accept him most willingly; it is a very fine and handsome present. May God make him a great man!"

He then sent for the most trusty equerry of his stables and gave into his charge young Bayard, with the assurance that one day he would do him great credit. The Bishop of Grenoble, having accomplished his business, did not tarry long after this, but having humbly thanked the Duke of Savoy, took leave of him and of his nephew, and returned to his own home.

Those spring and summer months spent at the Court of Savoy remained a happy memory to Bayard all his life. On feast-days and holidays the whole company would go out into the woods or the meadows, the Duchess Blanche with her young maidens and attendant ladies, while the knights and squires and pages waited upon them as they dined under the trees, and afterwards played games and made the air ring with their merry songs. Or there were hunting and hawking parties which lasted for more than one day, or river excursions down as far as the Lake of Bourget, where the Duke had a summer palace. It must have been on occasions such as these when the gallant young Bayard met with the maiden who caught his boyish fancy, and to whom he remained faithful at heart until the end of his days. Yet this pretty old-world story of boy-and-girl affection made no farther progress, and when the knight and lady met in the years to come, once more under the hospitable care of the good Duchess Blanche, they met as congenial friends only. The fair maiden of Chambery is known to history solely by her later married name of Madame de Frussasco (or Fluxas), and in the records of chivalry only by the tournament in which the "Good Knight without Fear and without Reproach" wore her colours and won the prize in her name.

CHAPTER II

The King heard that the Duke of Savoy was coming to his Court, and he sent the Comte de Ligny to conduct the Duke on his way, and to receive him with due honour. They met him about six miles from Lyons, and gave him a warm welcome, after which the two princes rode side by side, and had much talk together, for they were cousins and had not met for a long time. Now this Monseigneur de Ligny was a great general, and with his quick, observant eye he soon took notice of young Bayard, who was in the place of honour close to his lord, and he inquired: "Who is that gallant little lad riding his horse so well that it is quite a pleasure to see him?"

"Upon my word," replied the Duke, "I never had such a delightful page before. He is a nephew of the Bishop of Grenoble, who made me a present of him only six months ago. He was but just out of the riding-school, but I never saw a boy of his age distinguish himself so much either on foot or on horseback. And I may tell you, my lord and cousin, that he comes of a grand old race of brave and noble knights; I believe he will follow in their steps." Then he cried out to Bayard: "Use your spurs, my lad, give your horse a free course and show what you can do."

The lad did not want telling twice, and he gave such a fine exhibition of horsemanship that he delighted all the company. "On my honour, my lord, here is a young gentleman who has the making of a gallant knight," exclaimed de Ligny; "and in my opinion you had better make a present of both page and horse to the King, who will be very glad of them, for if the horse is good and handsome, to my mind the page is still better."

"Since this is your advice," replied Charles of Savoy, "I will certainly follow it. In order to succeed, the boy cannot learn in a better school than the Royal House of France, where honour may be gained better than elsewhere."

With such pleasant talk they rode on together into the city of Lyons, where the streets were full of people, and many ladies were looking out of the windows to see the coming of this noble prince and his gay company. That night the Duke gave a banquet in his own lodging, where the King's minstrels and singers entertained the guests, then there were games and pastimes, ending with the usual wine and spices being handed round, and at last each one retired to his own chamber until the dawn of day.

The next morning the Duke rose early and set forth to seek the King, whom he found on the point of going to Mass. The King greeted him at once most warmly and embraced him, saying, "My cousin, my good friend, you are indeed welcome, and if you had not come to me I should have had to visit you in your own country...." Then, after more polite talk, they rode together on their mules to the convent, and devoutly heard Mass, after which the King entertained the Duke of Savoy, Monsieur de Ligny, and other nobles to dinner with him, and they had much merry talk about dogs and falcons, arms and love-affairs. Presently de Ligny said to the King: "Sire, I give you my word that my lord of Savoy wishes to give you a page who rides his chestnut better than any boy I ever saw, and he cannot be more than fourteen, although his horsemanship is as good as that of a man of thirty. If it pleases you to go and hear vespers at Ainay you will have your pastime in the fields there afterwards." "By my faith," cried the King, "I do wish it!" and he heard the whole story of this wonderful boy from the Duke of Savoy.

When young Bayard heard that the King was to see him he was as much delighted as if he had won the city of Lyons; and he went in haste to the head groom of the Duke of Savoy and prayed him to get his horse ready for him, offering his short dagger as a present. But this the man refused and made reply: "Go and comb and clean yourself, my friend, and put on your best clothes, and if, by God's help, the King of France takes you in favour, you may some day become a great lord and be able to serve me." "Upon my faith! You may trust me never to forget all the kindness you have shown me," replied the boy; "and if God ever gives me good fortune you shall share it." It seemed a long time to his impatience before the hour arrived when he rode his horse, attended by his equerry, to the meadow where he was to await the King and his company, who arrived by boat on the Saone. As soon as Charles VIII. had landed he cried: "Page, my friend, touch up your horse with your spurs!"

which the lad did at once, and to see him you would have thought that he had been doing it all his life. At the end of his race Bayard made his clever horse take a few jumps, and then he rode straight towards the King and gracefully drew up before him with a low bow. All the company was delighted with the performance, and the King bade him do it again. "Picquez! Picquez!" (Prick up your horse!), he cried, and all the pages shouted: "Picquez! Picquez!" with enthusiasm, so that for some time the name stuck to him.

Then Charles turned to the Duke of Savoy and said: "I see that my cousin of Ligny told me the truth at dinner, and now I will not wait for you to give me this page and his horse, but I demand it of you as a favour."

"Most willingly, my lord," answered the Duke, "and may God give him grace to do you true service." After this young Bayard was given into the special charge of the lord of Ligny, who was greatly pleased and felt sure that he would make of him a noble knight.

Meantime, the Duke of Savoy remained for awhile at the Court of Charles VIII., with whom he was in great favour, and they were like brothers together. This young King was one of the best of princes, courteous, generous, and beloved of all men. At length the day of departure came, and the good Duke went back to his own country, laden with beautiful and honourable presents.

During three years young Bayard remained as a page in the service of the Seigneur de Ligny, being trained with the utmost care in all that would be needful to him in his profession of arms.

He won so much favour from his lord that at the early age of seventeen he was raised from his position as a page to that of a squire, and appointed man-at-arms in the General's company, being retained at the same time as one of the gentlemen of the household, with a salary of 300 livres. As a man-at-arms Bayard would have under him a page or varlet, three archers, and a soldier armed with a knife (called a "coutillier"). Thus, when we find a company of men-at-arms spoken of, it means for each "lance garnie," or man-at-arms, really six fighting men on horseback.

When King Charles VIII. found himself once more in his loyal city of Lyons, it chanced that a certain Burgundian lord, Messire Claude de Vauldray, a most famous man-at-arms, came to the King and proposed that he should hold a kind of tournament, called a "Pas d'Armes," to keep the young gentlemen of the Court from idleness. He meant by this a mimic attack and defence of a military position, supposed to be a "pas" or difficult and narrow pass in the mountains. It was a very popular test of chivalry, as the defender hung up his escutcheons on trees or posts put up for the purpose, and whoever wished to force this "pas" had to touch one of the escutcheons with his sword, and have his name inscribed by the King-at-arms in charge of them.

There was nothing that King Charles VIII. loved better than these chivalrous tournaments, and he gladly gave his consent. Messire Claude de Vauldray at once set about his preparations, and hung up his escutcheons within the lists which had been arranged for the coming tournament.

Young Bayard, whom every one called Picquet, passed before the shields and sighed with longing to accept the challenge and so improve himself in the noble science of arms. As he stood there silent and thoughtful, his companion, called Bellabre, of the household of the Sire de Ligny, asked him what he was thinking of. He replied: "I will tell you, my friend. It has pleased my lord to raise me from the condition of page into that of a squire, and I long to touch that shield, but I have no means of obtaining suitable armour and horses." Then Bellabre, a brave young fellow some years older than himself, exclaimed: "Why do you trouble about that, my companion? Have you not your uncle, that fat Abbe of Ainay? I vow that we must go to him, and if he will not give you money we must take his cross and mitre! But I believe that when he sees your courage he will willingly help you."

Bayard at once went and touched the shield, whereupon Mountjoy, King-at-arms, who was there to write down the names, began to reason with him. "How is this, Picquet, my friend; you will not be growing your beard for the next three years, and yet you think of fighting against Messire Claude, who is one of the most valiant knights of all France?" But the youth replied modestly: "Mountjoy, my friend, what I am doing is not from pride or conceit, but my only desire is to learn how to fight from those who can teach me. And if God pleases He will grant that I may do something to please the ladies." Whereupon Mountjoy broke out into a hearty laugh, which showed how much he enjoyed it.

The news soon spread through Lyons that Picquet had touched the shield of Messire Claude, and it came to the ears of the Sire de Ligny, who would not have missed it for ten thousand crowns. He went at once to tell the King, who was greatly delighted and said: "Upon my faith! Cousin de Ligny, your training will do you honour again, if my heart tells me true." "We shall see how it will turn out," was the grave reply; "for the lad is still very young to stand the attack of a man like Messire Claude."

But that was not what troubled young Bayard; it was the question how to find money for suitable horses and accoutrements. So he went to his companion, Bellabre, and asked for his help. "My friend, I beg of you to come with me to persuade my uncle, the Abbe of Ainay, to give me money. I know that my uncle, the Bishop of Grenoble, would let me want for nothing if he were here, but he is away at his Abbey of St. Sernin at Toulouse, which is so far off that there would be no time for a man to go there and back." "Do not trouble," said his friend, "you and I will go to Ainay, and I trust we shall manage it." This was some comfort, but the young warrior had no sleep that night. He and Bellabre, who shared the same bed, rose very early and took one of the little boats from Lyons to Ainay. On their arrival, the first person they met in the meadow was the Abbe himself, reading his prayers with one of his monks. The two young men advanced to salute him, but he had already heard of his nephew's exploit, and received him very roughly. "Who made you bold enough to touch the shield of Messire Claude?" he asked angrily. "Why, you have only been a page for three years, and you can't be more than seventeen or eighteen. You deserve to be flogged for showing such great pride." To which his nephew replied: "Monseigneur, I assure you that pride has nothing to do with it, but the desire and will to follow in the steps of your brave ancestors and mine. I entreat you, sir, that, seeing I have no other friends or kindred near, you will help me with a little money to obtain what is needful."

"Upon my word!" exclaimed the Abbe, "go and seek help elsewhere; the funds of my abbey are meant to serve God and not to be spent in jousts and tournaments." Bellabre now put in his word and remonstrated.

"Monseigneur, if it had not been for the virtue and the valour of your ancestors you would never have been Abbe of Ainay, for by their merits and not yours it was gained. Your nephew is of the same noble race, and well-beloved of the King; it is absolutely necessary that you should help him...." After more talk of this kind the Abbe at last consented, and took the two squires into his own room, where he opened a little cupboard, and from a purse which was inside he took out a hundred crowns and gave them to Bellabre, saying: "I give you this to buy two horses for this brave man-at-arms, for he has not enough beard to handle money himself. I will also write a line to Laurencin,[2] my tailor, to supply him with needful accoutrements." "You have done well, my lord," said Bellabre, "and I assure you that every one will honour you for this." When the young gentlemen had their letter they took leave with many humble thanks, and returned at once to Lyons in their little boat, highly pleased with their success.

"We are in good luck," said Bellabre, "and we must make the most of it. Let us go at once to the merchant before your good uncle changes his mind, for he will soon remember that he has put no limit to your expenses, and he can have no idea what a proper outfit will cost. You may be sure that you will never see any more of his money." So they took their boat on to the market-place, found the merchant at home, lost no time in telling of the good Abbe's generosity, and encouraged Laurencin to exert himself to the utmost in the way of splendid suits of clothing and armour, to do honour to his patron's gallant nephew, for there seemed to be no question of economy. Bayard was measured and fitted with cloth of silver, velvet, and satin, and then went gaily home with his friend, both of them thinking it an excellent jest.

When the Abbe of Ainay bethought himself later of what he had done, and sent a messenger in haste to the tailor, he found that it was too late and that his bill would come to hundreds of crowns. He was furious, and vowed that his nephew should never have another penny from him; but that did not mend matters, for the story got about, to the intense amusement of the King and his Court, and the rich old miser met with no sympathy.

The young men were fortunate enough to buy two excellent horses for much less than their value from a brave knight who had broken his leg, and not being able to figure in the contests himself, was willing to help so gallant a youth.

The time was drawing near for the great tournament, which would be a high festival for the town and was looked forward to with much eagerness and excitement. The course on which the knights were to fight was surrounded and duly laid out with richly-painted posts. At one side of this enclosed field, stands were put up and made very bright and gay with coloured hangings, carpets, embroidered ban-

---

2   The most important and wealthy merchant of Lyons.

ners, and escutcheons. It was here that the royal and noble company would sit and watch the proceedings.

Meantime, by permission of the King, Messire Claude de Vauldray had caused it to be published and declared throughout the city that he would hold the "pas" against all comers, both on foot and on horseback, on the approaching Monday.

A tournament was always a gorgeous and brilliant spectacle, but on this occasion, being held by the King's desire and graced by his presence, it was more splendid than usual. In our day, when it is the custom of men to avoid all show and colour in their dress, we can scarcely picture to ourselves the magnificence of those knights of the Renaissance. When the gallant gentleman actually entered the lists for fighting, he wore his suit of polished armour, often inlaid with gold or silver, a coloured silken scarf across his shoulders richly embroidered with his device, and on his head a shining helmet with a great tuft of flowing plumes. But in the endless stately ceremonies which followed or preceded the tournament, the knight wore his doublet of fine cloth, overlaid with his coat-of-arms embroidered in silk or gold thread, and an outer surcoat of velvet, often crimson slashed with white or violet satin, made without sleeves if worn over the cuirass and finished with a short fluted skirt of velvet. Over this a short cloak of velvet or satin, even sometimes of cloth of gold, was worn lightly over one shoulder.

If this was the usual style of costume, which had also to be varied on different festivals, we can easily understand how impossible it was for young Bayard to procure such costly luxuries on his small means, and we can almost forgive him for the audacious trick he played on his rich relation the Abbe of Ainay. Not only was the knight himself richly clad, but we are told that to appear in a grand tournament even the horse had to have sumptuous trappings of velvet or satin made by the tailor. We have not mentioned the suit of armour, which was the most expensive item of all; being made at this period lighter and more elaborate, with its flexible over-lying plates of thin, tempered steel, it was far more costly than it had ever been before. The bravest knights at the Court were proud to try their fortune against Messire Claude. It was the rule that after the contest each champion was to ride the whole length of the lists, with his visor raised and his face uncovered, that it might be known who had done well or ill. Bayard, who was scarcely eighteen and had not done growing, was by nature somewhat thin and pale, and had by no means reached his full strength. But with splendid courage and gallant spirit, he went in for his first ordeal against one of the finest warriors in the world. The old chronicler cannot tell how it happened, whether by the special grace of God or whether Messire Claude took delight in the brave boy, but it so fell out that no man did better in the lists, either on foot or on horseback, than young Bayard, and when it came to his turn to ride down with his face uncovered, the ladies of Lyons openly praised him as the finest champion of all. He also won golden opinions of all the rest of the company, and King Charles exclaimed at supper:

"By my faith! Picquet has made a beginning which in my opinion promises a good end." Then, turning to the Sire de Ligny, he added: "My cousin, I never in my life made you so good a present as when I gave him to you." "Sire," was the reply, "if he proves himself a worthy knight it will be more to your honour than mine, for it is your kind praise which has encouraged him to undertake such a feat of arms as this. May God give him grace to continue as he has begun." Then the General added, turning round with a smile to the assembled company:

"But we all know that his uncle, the Abbe of Ainay, does not take great pleasure in the youth's exploits, for it was at the old gentleman's expense that he procured his accoutrements." This remark was received with a roar of laughter, in which the King himself joined, for he had already heard the story and was very much amused at it. Soon after the tournament the Sire de Ligny sent for young Bayard one morning and said to him: "Picquet, my friend, you have begun with rare good fortune; you must carry on the pursuit of arms, and I retain you in my service with three hundred francs a year and three war-horses, for I have placed you in my company. Now I wish you to go to the garrison and meet your companions, assuring you that you will find as gallant men-at-arms there as any in Christendom; they often have jousts and tournaments to keep in practice of arms and acquire honour. It seems to me that while awaiting any rumour of war you cannot do better than stay there."

Bayard, who desired nothing more, replied: "My lord, for all the goods and honours which you have bestowed upon me I can only at this present time return you thanks.... My greatest desire is to go and join the company which you speak of, and if it is your good pleasure I will start to-morrow." "I am quite willing," said the Sire de Ligny; "but you must first take leave of the King, and I will bring you to him after dinner." Which was done, and the youth was thus presented: "Sire, here is your Picquet, who is going to see his companions in Picardy, and he is come to say good-bye to you." Young Bayard knelt before the King, who said to him with a smile: "Picquet, my friend, may God continue in you that which I have seen begun, and you will be a gallant knight; you are going into a country where there are fair ladies, be courteous and chivalrous to them, and farewell, my friend." After this, all the princes and lords crowded round to take leave of the young soldier, with much affection and regret at losing him. When he reached his lodging, he found that the King had sent him a purse of three hundred crowns, and also one of the finest war-horses in the royal stable. With his usual impulsive generosity Bayard gave handsome presents to the messengers, and then went to spend the evening with the Sire de Ligny, who treated him as though he were his own son, giving him wise advice for his future life, and above all bidding him keep honour always before his eyes. This command did he keep in very truth until his death. At last, when it grew late, de Ligny said to him: "Picquet, my friend, I think you will be starting to-morrow morning before I have risen, may God bless you!" and embraced him with tears, while Bayard on his knees said good-bye to his kind master.

More presents awaited him, for that night there arrived two complete and costly suits from the Sire de Ligny, who also sent his own favourite chestnut horse, so that when the young squire set forth at daybreak he was splendidly equipped in every way with horses, servants, armour, and clothes suitable to his position. As we have seen, dress was a very expensive thing in those days, when gentlemen of rank wore velvet, brocade, and satin, both for evening and riding costume as a matter of course.

It was a slow journey into Picardy, for Bayard wished his horses to arrive in good condition, and only travelled a moderate distance every day. When he arrived at the little town of Aire, his destination, all the young officers of the garrison came out to meet him, for the fame of his jousting with Messire Claude de Vauldray had already reached them. They would not listen to his modest disclaimers, but feasted and made much of their new comrade. One lively young noble of the company, probably quite deceived by the fine show that Bayard made with all his handsome parting gifts, and taking him for a man of wealth, said to him: "My good companion, you must make people talk about you, and endeavour to acquire the good favour of all the fair ladies of this country, and you cannot do better than give us a tournament, for it is a long time since we have had one in this town." The poor boy must have been somewhat taken aback by this suggestion, but he was far too plucky to show it, so he replied with ready goodwill, "On my faith, Monsieur de Tardieu, is that all? You may be sure that this will please me even more than yourself. If you will have the goodness to send me the trumpeter to-morrow morning, and if we have leave of our captain, I will take care that you shall be satisfied."

All that night Bayard was too excited to sleep, and when Tardieu came to his lodging in the morning with the trumpeter of the company, he had already settled exactly what he would do and had written out his announcement, which ran thus: "Pierre de Bayard, young gentleman and apprentice of arms, native of Dauphine, of the army of the King of France, under the high and puissant lord the Sire de Ligny--causeth to be proclaimed and published a tournament to be held outside the town of Aire, close to the walls, for all comers, on the 20th day of July. They are to fight with three charges of the lance without 'lice'" (meaning in this instance a barrier), "with sharpened point, armed at all points; afterwards twelve charges with the sword, all on horseback. And to him who does best will be given a bracelet enamelled with his arms, of the weight of thirty crowns. The next day there shall be fought on foot a charge with the lance, at a barrier waist-high, and after the lance is broken, with blows of the axe, until it is ended at the discretion of the judges and those who keep the camp. And to him who does best shall be given a diamond of the value of forty crowns."

This sounds more like real war than courtly pastime, and we see how terribly in earnest this young soldier was. The allusion to "those who keep the camp" is to the marshals of the tournament and the heralds-at-arms who kept a very close watch on the combatants. They also maintained on this miniature battlefield the laws of chivalry and courtesy, giving help to those who needed it.

When a young squire first entered the lists he was warned by the cry: "Remember of what race you come and do nothing contrary to your honour." There were many strict rules to be observed; for instance, it was forbidden to strike your adversary with the point, although it was usually blunted (but not in this tournament of Bayard's). It was forbidden to attack the horse of your opponent, and this we can quite understand, for in those days, when a knight wore complete and heavy armour, if his horse were killed he was absolutely at the mercy of his enemy.

It was always made a ground of complaint against the Spaniards that they attacked the horses of the foe. In a tournament it was the rule only to strike at the face or the chest, both well protected by the visor and the breastplate, and to cease at once if the adversary raised the visor of his helmet. Also no knight was to fight out of his rank when making a rush together. This was very important when the champions were divided into two companies under the order of two chiefs, and were placed exactly opposite each other, at the two ends of the arena. On a signal made by the marshals of the tournament, they charged impetuously upon each other, with their horses at full gallop. They held the lances straight out until the signal came, then lowering the lances, they rushed forward amid a cloud of dust with loud war-cries and the fight became a furious scuffle. The knights who had stood the first shock without being unhorsed or wounded, pressed forward and fought with the sword, until one of the marshals threw his wand of office into the arena to show that the contest was over.

In these tournaments the horses were frequently armed as well as their riders, and they were often gaily caparisoned with emblazoned housings, sometimes of very costly material, such as satin embroidered with gold or silver.

At the time when young Bayard joined his company at Aire, there were stationed in Picardy at no great distance about seven or eight hundred men-at-arms in these regulation companies (compagnies d'ordonnance) as they were called. When they were not actually employed on duty, they were very glad to take their pleasure in all sorts of warlike games. As we may suppose, they were delighted to take part in the proposed tournament. Amongst these companies there were some of the famous Scotch Guards, who had first been taken into the service of France by Charles VII.

The time fixed was only eight days off, but all the same about forty or fifty men-at-arms gave in their names. Fortunately, before the expected day, that gentle knight, the Captain Louis d'Ars, arrived, and he was much delighted to have come in time for this entertainment. When Bayard heard of his captain's arrival he went to pay his respects to him at once, and was most warmly welcomed, for the boy's fame had gone before him. To make the festival more complete, his friend Bellabre also appeared, having been delayed by waiting for two splendid horses which he expected from Spain. At length the eventful day arrived, and the gentlemen who wished to take part in the tournament were divided into two equal ranks, there being twenty-three on one side and twenty-three on the other. The judges chosen were the Captain Louis d'Ars and the lord of St. Quentin, captain of the Scotch company.

At this point it will be interesting to give a full account of the details needful for a tournament of this period, the close of the fifteenth century. These tournaments were first started as training-schools for the practice of arms, and were later tempered by the rules of chivalry. Jousts were single combats, often a succession of them, for a prize or trial of skill, while the tourney was troop against troop. These warlike games were very popular in France especially, but very strict rules had to be made to prevent the "joust of peace" becoming the deadly "joust a l'outrance" (to the death).

The "lists," or tournament grounds, were in Bayard's time usually of a square shape rather longer than broad, and were surrounded by palisades, often adorned with tapestry and heraldic devices. The marshals of the lists took note of all that happened and enforced the rules of chivalry. Varlets were in attendance to help the esquires in looking after their masters, and helping them up, with their heavy armour, if unhorsed.

It was common to hold a "passage of arms" for three days: two for the contest on horseback, first with lances, second with swords and maces; while on the third day, on foot, pole-axes were used. A specially heavy kind of armour was worn, sometimes nearly 200 lbs. in weight, so that a knight once unhorsed lay on the ground absolutely helpless, and could not rise without help. This armour was made still stronger by "reinforcing armour"--pieces screwed on over the left side, chiefly, which received most blows--making a double defence for the head, chest, and left shoulder. "Pauldrons" or shoulder-guards buckled on, that on the right arm being smaller to leave freedom for using the lance. Then we have brassards or arm-guards; the rere-brace for the upper arm, the vam-brace for the lower, and the elbow-piece called a "coudiere."

When all was ready on the appointed day for the tournament at Aire, the trumpet sounded, and then the order of the Tourney was declared aloud. Bayard had to appear first in the lists, and against him rode forth a neighbour of his in Dauphine, by name Tartarin, a powerful man-at-arms. They rushed at each other so vehemently that Tartarin broke his lance half a foot from the iron, and Bayard struck him above the arm-piece of his armour and broke his lance into five or six pieces, upon which the trumpets sounded forth triumphantly, for the joust was wonderfully good. After having finished their first attack they returned to face each other for the second. Such was the fortune of Tartarin that with his lance he forced in Bayard's arm-piece, and every one thought that he had his arm pierced. But he was not hurt, and succeeded in returning the attack by a stroke above the visor, which carried off the bunch of plumes from his adversary's helmet. The third bout with the lance was as good or even better than the others, for the lance was more completely shivered into fragments.

When these two knights had finished, next came the lord of Bellabre, and against him a Scotch man-at-arms, named the Captain David of Fougas, and these likewise did with their three jousts of the lance all that it was possible for gentlemen to do. Thus, two by two, all the company went through the same contest.

This jousting with the lance was one of the most popular exercises for knights of that day, and the proper use of this weapon was one of the most important accomplishments for a warrior. We shall often notice, in the accounts of Bayard's adventures on the field of battle, how extremely expert he was with his lance. The supreme triumph with this weapon was to use such skill and force as to break the lance shaft--made of ash or sycamore--into as many pieces as possible; in fact, to "shiver" it completely, and thus break as many lances as possible. The tilting lance was often made hollow, and was from 12 to 15 feet long; but the lance used with the object of unhorsing instead of splintering was much stronger, heavier, and thicker in the stem, and instead of a pointed head had a "coronal," which was blunt.

The first part of the tournament having come to an end, then followed the battle of the swords. According to the rules, this began with Bayard, who, on the third stroke he gave, broke his sword into two pieces, but he made such good use of the stump that he went through the number of strokes commanded, and did his duty so well that no man could have done better. After this came the others according to their order, and for the rest of that day there was such a succession of vigorous fighting that the two judges declared "never had there been finer lance work or contests with the sword." When the evening came they retired to young Bayard's lodging, where a great supper was prepared, to which came many ladies, for within ten miles round all those of Picardy, or the greater number, had come to see this fine tournament. After the supper there were dances and other entertainments, and the company was so well amused that it struck one hour after midnight before they broke up. It was late next morning before they woke up, and you may believe that they were never weary of praising Messire de Bayard, as much for his skill at arms as for his good hospitality.

The next morning, in order to complete that which had begun so well, all the soldiers assembled at the dwelling of their Captain Louis d'Ars, where Bayard had already arrived, having come to invite him to dinner at his lodging, in company with the ladies of the previous evening. First they all went to hear Mass, and when that was over, "you should have seen the young gentlemen taking the ladies' arms, and with much pleasant talk leading them to Bayard's lodging, where if they had supped well the night before, at dinner they did still better." There was no lingering after this meal, and towards two o'clock all those who were to take part in the second day's tournament retired to arm themselves and make ready to fight. The combatants all approached on horseback, and gravely went round to salute the company before the contest began.

It was Bayard's place to begin, and against him came a gentleman from Hainault, Hannotin de Sucker, of great repute. They fought with their lances, one on each side of the barrier, and gave such tremendous strokes that the lances were soon broken to pieces; after this they took their battle-axes, which each of them had hanging by their sides, and dealt each other great and terrible blows. This appears to us an extremely rough form of entertainment, but we must remember that these knights were clad in armour, and so thoroughly covered up from head to foot that there was not supposed to be a place where a pin could pierce between the joints of the armour. Under the helmet a smaller close-fitting steel cap was often worn. This fierce contest went on until Bayard gave his opponent a blow near the ear, which caused him to waver, and worse still, to fall on his knees, when, pursuing his success, the victor charged again over the barrier, and caused Hannotin to kiss the ground.

When the judges saw this they cried, "Hola! Hola! that is enough; now you may retire." After these two came Bellabre and Arnaulton of Pierre Forade, a gentleman of Gascony, who did wonders with their lances until they were both broken; and then they came to the battle-axes, but Bellabre broke his, after which the judges parted them. After these two came Tardieu and David the Scotchman, and they did their duty very well. So did others in turn, so that it was seven o'clock before it was all finished and, for a small tournament, the lookers-on never saw better jousting in their lives.

When all was over, each man went to his lodging to disarm and change; then they all came to Bayard's lodging, where the banquet was ready, and there were also the two judges, the lords of Ars and of St. Quentin, and all the ladies. After supper it had to be decided and declared by the judges who should have the prizes. Some of the gentlemen most experienced in arms were asked to give their opinion "on their faith," and afterwards the ladies on their conscience, without favouring one more than another. At last it was agreed that, although each one had done his duty well, yet in their judgment during the two days Messire de Bayard had done best of all; wherefore they left it to him, as the knight who had gained the prizes, to give his presents where it seemed good to him. There was a discussion between the judges as to who should pronounce sentence, but the Captain Louis d'Ars persuaded the lord of St. Quentin to do so.

The trumpet was sounded to command silence, and St. Quentin said: "My lords who are here assembled, and especially those who have been in the Tourney of which Messire Pierre Bayard has given the prizes for two days ... we would have you know that after due inquiry of the virtuous and brave gentlemen who were present and saw the contests, and of the noble ladies here present ... we have found that although each one has very well and honestly done his duty, yet the common voice is that the lord of Bayard has done best in these two days; wherefore the lords and ladies leave to him the honour of giving the prizes where it seems good to him." Then he added: "My lord of Bayard, decide where you will give them." The young knight blushed modestly and was quite troubled. Then he said:

"My lord, I do not know why this honour should come to me, for I think that others have deserved it more than I. But as it pleases the lords and ladies that I should be judge, I hope that the gentlemen, my companions, will not be displeased if I give the prize for the first day to my lord of Bellabre, and for the second day to the Captain David of Scotland." He therefore gave the gold bracelet to his friend Bellabre, and the diamond to the Scotch Captain David, and his decision was greatly applauded. There was again feasting and dancing afterwards, and the ladies could not say enough in praise of their gallant young host. We may imagine the penniless condition in which all this extravagant generosity left him, but his extreme liberality appears to have been one great feature of his character which made him beloved through life by all who had to do with him.

He never could see one of his companions thrown without giving him another horse; if he had a crown left, every one shared it. He never refused the request of any man if he could possibly grant it, and in his gifts was always gentle and courteous. His chronicler makes a special point of his piety from early youth; the first thing when he rose in the morning was always a prayer to God, as he had promised his mother.

CHAPTER III

During two years Bayard remained with the garrison at Aire, and made great progress in all warlike training. At the end of this time, in the year 1494, Charles VIII. undertook his first expedition to Italy, and as the company of the Count de Ligny was commanded to join him, young Bayard looked forward with great delight to his first taste of real warfare.

The young King of France, in his eager desire for military glory, forsook the wise policy of his father, Louis XI., and resolved to claim the kingdom of Naples, in assertion of the rights bequeathed to him by Rene of Anjou. In order to prevent any opposition from Spain he yielded to King Ferdinand the provinces of Roussillon and Cerdagne, and on the same principle gave up to the Emperor Maximilian, Artois and Franche-Comte. Having made these real sacrifices as the price of a doubtful neutrality, he set forth on his wild dreams of conquest at a distance, which could be of no permanent advantage to him.

Charles VIII. had soon collected a magnificent army and crossed the Alps in August 1494; it was composed of lances, archers, cross-bow men, Swiss mercenaries, and arquebusiers. These last used a kind of hand-gun which had only been in common use for about twenty years, since the battle of Morat. The arquebus had a contrivance, suggested by the trigger of the cross-bow, to convey at once the burning match to the trigger. Before that the match had been held in the hand in using the hand-gun as well as the hand-cannon. Many of these arquebusiers were on horseback. Besides a number of small pieces of artillery, the French army had 140 big cannons. The use of these fire-arms in war had been gradually increasing since the days when Louis XI. made such use of his "bombards" in the wars in Flanders.

When we read of the wonderful success which at first attended the French army, we must remember how greatly superior it was to the troops which opposed it in Italy, which were mostly bands of adventurers collected by mercenary leaders, named Condottieri, who fought for gain rather than for glory, and had no special zeal or loyalty for the prince who employed them. The soldiers in their pay were, for the time being, their own personal property, and their great desire was to save them "to fight another day," while it was not to their interest to kill the men of another band (who might be on the same side next time), and they only sought to make prisoners for the sake of their ransom. The impetuosity and real warlike spirit of the French was a new and alarming thing in Italy, which had been so long accustomed to the mere show of war.

Charles passed as a conqueror through Pisa and Florence to Rome, then victorious at Capua, he entered Naples in triumph. During the spring months of 1495, spoilt by his easy victory, he gave himself up to pleasure in that fair southern land, idly dreaming of distant conquest. His success awakened the jealous alarm of Europe, and a formidable league was formed against him by all the Italian States, the Emperor Maximilian, and the Kings of Spain and England. Suddenly roused to a sense of his danger, Charles VIII. left his new kingdom in the charge of his cousin, Gilbert de Montpensier, with a few thousand men, and hastily set forth on his homeward way. He left garrisons in various conquered cities, and his army consisted of barely 10,000 men. They crossed the Apennines with great labour and difficulty, to find their passage barred by the confederates on the Emilian plain near the village of Fornovo.

Never was battle more fiercely contested than on that Monday, 6th July, when the French succeeded in breaking through the host of their enemies. The actual fighting lasted little more than an hour, amid a scene of the wildest confusion, which was increased by a storm of thunder and lightning, with rain falling in torrents. We are told that Bayard, the Good Knight, who had accompanied the King through the whole campaign, distinguished himself in the first charge at the head of de Ligny's company, and had two horses killed under him, then continued fighting on foot, and in the thick of the battle he took the standard of the horsemen opposing him, and covered himself with glory. The King, hearing afterwards of his gallant deed, sent him a present of five hundred crowns. Charles could appreciate a kindred spirit as he too fought with splendid courage on that eventful day. The French camp, with all its rich treasures of armour, gorgeous clothing, rare tapestries and plate, was looted; but Charles VIII. and the greater part of his army, with all the artillery, made good their passage through an overwhelming host of foes and raised the siege of Novara, where Lodovico Sforza was besieging the Duke of Orleans.

The French King was soon to receive news of the defeat and destruction of the small army he had left to hold Naples, and the death of the gallant Viceroy, Gilbert de Montpensier. Such was the sad ending of the first of those glorious and fatal expeditions to Italy, in which four kings wasted in vain so much treasure and so many precious lives. Charles VIII. did not long survive this bitter disappointment. He died at Amboise on 7th April 1498, at the age of twenty-eight. As he left no children he was succeeded by his cousin, the Duke of Orleans, under the name of Louis XII. Louis XII. was crowned on the 1st of July 1498.

If there was one trait of character which, more than any other, distinguished Bayard the Good Knight, it was his absolute loyalty towards the lord he served, and his undying gratitude for any kindness which he had received. He never forgot those six happy months he had spent at the Court of Savoy when he first went there to take up the profession of arms as a young lad of thirteen. It was not by his own choice that he left the service of his earliest master, who in a fit of generosity had presented his favourite page to the King, in the hope that by so doing he would best further the career of Bayard.

But Charles I., Duke of Savoy, did not live to see this, for he had died in 1490, and the Duchess, his widow, had left Chambery and retired to her dower house in the pleasant town of Carignano, in Piedmont, about seventeen miles to the south of Turin. This lady, Blanche Paleologus, had been a most kind friend to young Bayard, and when she heard that he was stationed in the neighbourhood, she invited him to visit her, and received him with the utmost courtesy, treating him as if he were a member of her family. She was greatly beloved and honoured in Carignano, where she was lady suzerain, and where there may still be seen, in the church of Santa Maria delle Grazie, a splendid monument to her memory.

We may imagine the satisfaction with which the good Duchess found that her page of bygone days had blossomed out into a valiant and famous knight, and they must both have had much to hear and tell of all that had happened since they parted. Here Bayard also met with another friend, the young lady who had been one of the maids-of-honour of the Duchess at Chambery and who had won the boyish affection of the Good Knight. If the young folks had been able to follow their inclinations it is probable that in time to come, when they were of suitable age, marriage would have followed, so the "Loyal Servitor" tells us in his chronicle. But circumstances parted them, as Bayard went to the King's Court, and the fair maiden was married later to a very good and honourable gentleman, the Seigneur de Frussasco (or Fluxas), who was governor of the household to the Duchess of Savoy, a man of wealth and high position.

We have a simple, touching story of the delight with which the lady of Frussasco welcomed her dear friend, the Good Knight, of their eager talk about old times, and their high ideal of honour and duty. She told him how she had followed the story of his achievements, from his first joust with Messire Claude de Vauldray, his tournament at Aire in Picardy, and the honour which he received on the day of Fornovo, which had spread his fame throughout France and Italy, and she gave him so much praise and honour that the poor gentleman blushed for very shame.

Then the lady said to him: "Monseigneur de Bayard, my friend, this is the great house in which you were first brought up; would it not be well for you to distinguish yourself here as you have done so nobly elsewhere?"

The Good Knight made answer: "Madame, you know how from my youth I have always loved and honoured you, and I hold you to be so wise and so kind that you would only advise me for my good. Tell me, therefore, if you please, what you would have me do to give pleasure to my good mistress, the Duchess Blanche, to you above all, and to the rest of the noble company here at this time?"

Then the lady of Frussasco said: "It seems to me, my lord of Bayard, that you would do well to arrange some tournament in this town for the honour of Madame of Savoy, who will be very grateful to you. You have here in the neighbourhood many French gentlemen, your companions, and there are other gentlemen of this country who I am assured would all most willingly join you."

"If it is your wish," replied the Good Knight, "it shall be done. You are the one lady in this world who has first conquered my heart by your grace and kindness.... I pray of you that you will give me one of the under-sleeves from your dress, as I have need of it."[3] The lady gave it him, and he put it into the sleeve of his doublet without a word.

---

3   This was fastened with a little lacing under the hanging sleeve, and was the usual favour asked for and worn by the knight on his helmet.

The Duchess Blanche was never weary of talking with the Good Knight, who had always been so great a favourite of hers. But Bayard could not sleep all that night, for his mind was full of plans for carrying out the request of his lady. When the morning came he sent a trumpeter round to all the towns of the neighbourhood where there were garrisons, to make known to the gentlemen that if they would make their way within four days, on the next Sunday, to the town of Carignano, in the costume of men-at-arms, he would give a prize, which was the cuff of his lady, from whence hung a ruby of the value of a hundred ducats, to him who should be victorious in three encounters with the lance, without a barrier, and twelve turns with the sword.

On the appointed day, about an hour after noon, the Good Knight was at his place in the ranks, armed at all points, with three or four of his companions, but only those were with him who were prepared to take part in the coming contest. Bayard began first, and against him came the lord of Rovastre, a gallant gentleman who bore the ensign of the Duke Philibert of Savoy. He was a very hardy and skilful knight, who gave a fine thrust with his lance to begin with, but the Good Knight gave him such a blow on the broad band, which protected his right arm, that he disarmed him, and caused his lance to fly in five or six pieces. The lord of Rovastre regained his band and tilted with the second lance, with which he did his duty thoroughly ... but the Good Knight struck him on the visor, and carried off his plume of feathers (panache) and made him tremble, although he kept his seat on horseback. At the third lance the lord of Rovastre missed his aim, and Bayard broke his lance, which went to pieces.

After them came Mondragon and the lord of Chevron, who did their tilting so well that everybody applauded. Then came two others, and so on until all the company were satisfied.

The lances being broken it was now time for the contest with swords; but the Good Knight had only struck two blows when he broke his own, and sent that of his opponent flying out of his hand. The gracious Duchess requested the lord of Frussasco to invite all the gentlemen who had taken part in the tournament to supper. After supper the hautboys sounded, and the minstrels began to tune up in the gallery, but before the dancing began, it was decided to award the prize to him who had gained it. The lords of Grammont and Frussasco were the judges, and they asked all the company--gentlemen, ladies, and the combatants themselves--and they were all of opinion that the Good Knight himself, by right of arms, had gained the prize. But when they presented it to him he said that he did not deserve it, but that if he had done anything well, Madame de Frussasco was the cause, as she had lent him her sleeve, and that it was her place to give the prize as she chose.

The lady, who was well versed in the laws of honour and chivalry, humbly thanked the Good Knight for the honour which he had done her, and said: "As M. de Bayard has shown me this courtesy I will keep the sleeve all my life for love of him, while as for the ruby, I advise that it should be given to M. de Mondragon, for he is considered to have done the next best."

This was accomplished as she wished, to the content of all, and the Duchess Blanche rejoiced greatly in the success of the Good Knight, who had begun his career in her household. The Good Knight took leave of his noble mistress, the lady of Savoy, telling her that he owed her service and obedience next to the King, his sovereign lord. Then he said farewell to the lady who had been his first love, and they parted with much regret, but their warm friendship lasted till death. We do not hear that they ever met again, but not a year passed without presents being sent from one to the other.

CHAPTER IV

While the French army felt such absolute security of their dominion in Italy as to suffer the young captains to join in amusements, the fugitive Duke Lodovico Sforza of Milan, who had lost his duchy by treachery, was watching events and preparing to return.

When Lodovico arrived he was received with acclamation, and entered Milan in triumph.

If this sudden revolution took all Italy by surprise, we can understand the dismay of Louis XII., who found that he had all his work to do over again. For not only had Milan rebelled, but all the other towns which he had conquered.

King Louis sent the Sire de Ligny as his chief general, and as a matter of course the Good Knight went with him. I must tell you the story of an adventure he had. He was in a garrison about twenty miles from Milan with other young men-at-arms, and they were constantly making small expeditions. One day Bayard heard that in the little town of Binasco, near the Certosa di Pavia, there were about three hundred good horses, which he thought might be easily taken, and therefore he begged his companions to join him in this adventure. He was so much beloved that forty or fifty gentlemen gladly accompanied him. But the castellan of the fortress at Binasco had news of this through his spies, and laid a trap for the Frenchmen; he had a strong troop placed in ambuscade on the road, and made sure of success. But, though taken by surprise, the Good Knight fought like a lion, and with cries of "France! France!" led his little company again and again to the attack, for, as he told them, if news of this reached Milan not one would escape. In fact, so fierce was their charge that they drove back the defenders mile after mile to the very gates of Milan. Then one of the older soldiers, who saw the enemy's plan, shouted, "Turn, men-at-arms, turn!" and the others heard in time, but the Good Knight, thinking only of pursuing his foes, entered pell-mell with them into the city, and followed them to the very palace of the lord Lodovico. As he was wearing the white cross of France, he was soon surrounded on all sides and taken prisoner. Lodovico had heard the cries, and sent for this brave foe, who was disarmed before being taken to the palace.

The Duke of Milan was surprised to see such a young warrior, and asked him what brought him into the city. The Good Knight, who was never put out by any-thing, replied, "By my faith, my lord, I did not think I was coming in alone, but believed my companions were following me. They understood war better than I did, otherwise they would have been prisoners as I am...." Then Lovodico asked him how big was the French army, and he made answer, "As far as I know, my lord, there must be fourteen or fifteen hundred men-at-arms and sixteen or eighteen thousand men on foot; but they are all picked men, quite determined to win back the State of Milan for the King, our master. And it seems to me, my lord, that you would be much safer in Germany than you are here, for your men are not fit to fight us."

He spoke with so much confidence that Lodovico was much amused, and re-marked that he should like to see the two armies face to face. "And so indeed should I, my lord, if I were not a prisoner." "Really, if that is all," replied the Duke, "I will at once set you free, and make it up to the captain who took you prisoner. But tell me, if you desire anything else I will give it to you."

The Good Knight bent his knee in thanks for this generous offer, and replied: "My lord, I ask nothing else save that of your courtesy you will be good enough to return to me my horse and my arms which I brought into this town; and if you will send me to my garrison, which is twenty miles from here, you will thus render me a great service, for which I shall be grateful all my life; and saving my honour and the service of my King, I would do anything you command in return."

"On my faith!" exclaimed the lord Lodovico, "you shall have what you ask for at once." Then he turned to the Seigneur Jean Bernardin who had taken him pris-oner. "Do you hear, captain, he is to have his horse, his arms, and all his accoutre-ments at once"

"My lord," was the reply, "that is a very easy matter for all is at my lodging." So he sent two or three servants, who brought the horse, and the armour, which the

Duke caused to be put on before him. This arming took place in the great court-yard, at least as far as the gallant prisoner was disarmed, and when Bayard was fully accoutred he sprang on his horse without touching the stirrup, and asked for his lance, which was given him--a steel-headed weapon about fourteen feet long, the shaft being of ash or sycamore with a little flag (pennoncelle) waving at the top. Then, raising his visor, he said to the Duke: "My lord, I thank you for the great courtesy you have shown me. May God repay you!"

The Good Knight spurred his horse, who pranced about in the most wonder-ful way, and then Bayard gave a small exhibition of his skill with the lance which amazed the bystanders and did not please the lord Lodovico overmuch, for he re-marked: "If all the French men-at-arms were like this one I should have a poor chance." However, he took gracious leave of the Good Knight, and sent him forth with a trumpeter in attendance to conduct him back to his garrison.

They had not gone very far, only about twelve miles from Milan, when they met the main body of the French army. Every one was greatly surprised to see Bayard, for there had been great sorrow at the rumour that the gallant knight had been too rash and had been taken prisoner through his youthful boldness and rash-ness. When he reached the camp he found that the news of his exploit had preceded him, for the Sire de Ligny, his good leader, came forward to meet him with a smile, saying: "Hallo! Picquet, who has got you out of prison? Have you paid your ransoms' I was on the point of sending one of my trumpeters to pay it and fetch you back."

"My lord," replied the Good Knight, "I thank you humbly for your good will; but the lord Lodovico set me free by his great courtesy."

It was at Novara that Lodovico Sforza met the army of France. The Duke's forc-es were composed of different races--German "landsknechte," Burgundians who were commanded by the same Claude de Vauldray who had fought with the Good Knight in his first tournament, and Swiss mercenaries. There were bands of Swiss fighting on the side of the French, and those within the city declared that they would not fight against their fellow-countrymenn in the other camp. They laid down their arms, and neither threat nor promise availed. Soon it was discovered that one of the gates of Novara had been opened by treachery, and that the French were entering the city. Then, as a last hope, Lodovico and his companions put on the dress of common soldiers and mixed with them in the ranks. But the unfortunate Duke was betrayed by one of the Swiss captains, who was put to death later by his own countrymen as a traitor.

On the occasion of Louis' former conquest of this land he had given several important towns and estates to his general, the Sire de Ligny. These had revolted with the rest of the duchy, to the great annoyance of de Ligny, and a report reached the citizens of Tortona and Voghera that their homes were to be sacked and pillaged. This was of course in those days the usual penalty of rebellion, but the French general was a generous and merciful man who had no such cruel intentions. However, the inhabitants of Voghera took counsel together, and twenty of the chief merchants went forth to meet their lord and humbly pray for mercy, two miles outside the city gates. But de Ligny took no notice of them and rode on in silence with his men-at-arms to his lodging within the city. One of his captains, to whom they appealed, Louis d'Ars, promised to do his best for them, and advised that they should plead again on the morrow. This time about fifty of the chief men came to him as suppliants, bare-headed, and fell on their knees before the General. They made a long and lamentable petition, ending with the offer of the richest silver plate, cups, goblets, bowls, and precious vessels to the value of more than three hundred marks.

Without deigning to look at the presents they had brought, their offended lord turned upon them, reproached them bitterly for their treachery in rebelling against him before the usurper, Lodovico, had even approached their walls. What fate was too terrible for such cowards and traitors? The kneeling citizens trembled and thought their last hour had come, when the captain, Louis d'Ars, pleaded for mercy as a special favour to himself, promising that henceforth they would prove themselves faithful and loyal subjects. Then at length de Ligny suffered his anger to cool down, and yielded to the wish of his good captain by granting a pardon. "But as for your present, I do not deign to accept it for you are not worthy," he exclaimed. Then, looking round the hall, his eyes fell upon the Good Knight, to whom he said: "Picquet, take all this plate, I give it you for your kitchen." To which he made instant reply: "My lord, I thank you humbly for your kindness, but with God's help the goods of such evil-doers shall never enter my house for they would bring me misfortune."

Thereupon the Good Knight took one piece of silver after another from the table and made a present of it to each one of the assembled company, not keeping a single thing for himself, to the amazement of every one. When he had given away everything, he quietly left the chamber, as did many of the others. The Sire de Ligny turned to those who remained and asked: "What do you think of this, gentlemen? Did you ever see such a generous soul as my Picquet? God should have made him king over some great realm. Believe me that he will some day be one of the most perfect knights in the world." All the company agreed, and could not praise young Bayard enough. And when the Sire de Ligny had thought over the matter, he sent him next morning a beautiful costume of crimson velvet lined with satin brocade, a most excellent war-horse, and a purse with three hundred crowns--which did not last him long, for he shared it all with his companions.

Louis XII. had been so much engaged with his conquest of Milan that for a time he had not done much towards recovering the kingdom of Naples. This had been lost after the retreat of Charles VIII., who died before he had been able to make another fight for it, after the disastrous fate of his viceroy, Gilbert de Montpensier, and his brave little army. At this time Frederick of Aragon was King of Naples, having succeeded his nephew, Ferdinand II., in 1496.

The king gave the command of his great army to the lord of Aubigny, who had brought back the broken ranks of the first expedition to Naples. The company of de Ligny, under his lieutenant, Captain Louis d'Ars, was ordered to form part of it. Bayard, the Good Knight, who could not bear to be left behind when fighting was going on, asked the permission of his dear master to accompany the lieutenant's men.

On this important occasion Louis XII., doubtful of his own strength, made the great mistake of forming an alliance with Ferdinand, King of Spain.

King Frederick of Naples knew nothing of the secret compact between France and Spain, and he expected Gongalvo de Cordova, known as the Great Captain, to come to his help with the troops of Spain.

As the alliance between France and Spain was founded on treachery, we cannot be surprised that they soon fell out over the division of their spoils. King Ferdinand of Aragon was never bound by any contract which did not profit him, and by his orders the Great Captain, Gonzalvo de Cordova, invaded the province of Naples itself. The lord of Aubigny had placed his various companies as garrisons in different towns, and those which belonged to the Count de Ligny were in the hands of his company, amongst whom, as we know, was Bayard, the Good Knight. We shall now understand how it was that he found himself at war with the Spaniards, who had been at first the allies of France.

Pierre de Bayard, the Good Knight, had been placed in command of a garrison at a place called Monervine, by his captain, Louis d'Ars. There had been no fighting in his neighbourhood for some little time, and he began to get rather weary. So he said one evening to his companions: "Gentlemen, it seems to me that we have been too long in one place without seeing our foes. We shall grow weak for want of using our arms, and our enemies will grow bolder than ever, thinking that we dare not go out of our fort. So I propose that to-morrow we ride out towards the nearest Spanish garrisons, Andria or Barletta, and have a little fighting if possible." The others readily agreed, and about thirty of them arranged to start early the next morning. It was a merry party of young gentlemen who galloped over the country at daybreak, and it so chanced that the same idea had occurred to a Spanish knight of Andria, Don Alonzo of Soto-Mayor, who wished to exercise his company of men-at-arms. Such was the fortune of the two captains, that as they turned a corner by some rising ground they suddenly came within arrow-shot of each other, and joyful indeed they were to have such a chance. When the Good Knight saw the red crosses he turned to his followers and cried: "My friends, here is our chance to win honour ... we will not wait for them to attack!"

With a shout of delight they all lowered their visors, and crying, "***France, France***!" they galloped forward and charged their foes, who came proudly on to meet them with the cry of "***Spain! St. Iago***!" gaily receiving them on the point of their lances. In the shock of this first meeting many on both sides were borne to earth. The combat lasted a good half-hour before either side seemed to have the best of it, for they were well matched in numbers and strength. But in the end one side must win, and it chanced that the courage and skill of the Good Knight, and the enthusiasm with which he inspired his men, at last succeeded in breaking the ranks of the Spaniards, of whom about seven were killed and the same number taken prisoner, while the rest took to flight, and amongst them their captain, Don Alonzo. The Good Knight pursued, crying out to him: "Turn, man-at-arms, it would be a shame to die while running away." Presently Alonzo, like a fierce lion, turned against his pursuer with terrible force; and they fought desperately with sword-thrusts.

At length the horse of Don Alonzo backed and refused to advance any more, when the Good Knight, seeing that all the other Spaniards were gone, leaving their captain alone, said, "Surrender, man-at-arms, or you are dead." "To whom must I surrender?" he asked. "To the Captain Bayard," was the reply. Then Don Alonzo, who had already heard of that famous name, and knew that he had no chance of escape, gave up his sword and was taken with the other prisoners to the garrison, where with his usual chivalrous courtesy, the Good Knight gave Don Alonzo one of the best rooms of the castle, and supplied him with all that he needed, on receiving his parole that he would make no attempt to escape.

The Spanish captain was treated with the greatest kindness, being suffered to join in all the doings of the other gentlemen, and his ransom was fixed at 1000 crowns. But after a fortnight or more he grew tired of this life and persuaded an Albanian in the garrison to procure him a horse and help him to gain his freedom, for it was only fifteen or twenty miles to his own quarters. The man agreed, tempted by a high bribe, and Don Alonzo, who was allowed to come and go as he pleased, had no difficulty in passing out through the gateway in the early morning, when he and his companion put spurs to their horses and felt assured of success. But if the Good Knight was courteous he was not careless, and when he paid his usual morning call on his prisoner he was nowhere to be found. The watch was sounded, and the absence of the Albanian was also discovered, whereupon Bayard sent off in instant pursuit and Don Alonzo was overtaken within two miles of Andria, where he had dismounted to fasten the girth of his saddle which was broken. The Albanian managed to reach the Spanish quarter, for he knew that the penalty of his treachery would be hanging, and the Spanish knight was brought back to Monervine.

When Bayard met him he said: "How is it that you have broken your faith, my lord Don Alonzo? I will trust you no more, for it is not a knightly deed to escape from a place when you are on parole." The prisoner tried to excuse himself by vowing that he only went to fetch his ransom as he was troubled by receiving no news of his own people. But this did not avail him much, for he was kept in close confinement in a tower, but otherwise very well treated in the way of food and drink. After about another fortnight a trumpeter arrived to announce that the ransom was coming, and when this was duly paid, Don Alonzo took a friendly leave of his captors, having had time to notice that the Good Knight kept not a penny of the money for himself, but divided it all amongst his soldiers.

But the story does not end here, for this recreant knight was ungrateful enough to complain to his friends in the most outrageous manner of the treatment which he had received during his captivity. When this came to the knowledge of the Good Knight he was justly indignant, as were all his companions, and he at once wrote a letter to Don Alonzo, calling upon him to withdraw these untrue words, or to accept a challenge to mortal combat. This he sent by a trumpeter, and also offered his foe the choice of weapons, and whether the contest should be on foot or on horseback.

The Spanish captain sent back an insolent answer, saying that he would not withdraw anything he had said, and that he would prove his words in mortal combat within twelve days, two miles from the walls of Andria. In fixing this date he knew that Bayard was ill at the time with a quartan fever. But the Good Knight would not let such a small matter interfere with his knightly honours, and when the day arrived he rode to the spot appointed, with the Sire de la Palisse and his friend Bellabre as his seconds, and about two hundred men-at-arms as a guard of honour.

Bayard was clothed in white as a mark of humility and rode a splendid horse, but as Don Alonzo had not appeared, a trumpeter was sent to hasten his coming. When he was told that the Good Knight was on horseback with the usual armour, he exclaimed: "How is this? I was to choose the arms. Trumpeter, go and tell him that I will fight on foot." He said this, thinking that the illness of Bayard would make it quite impossible for him; and the trumpeter was greatly surprised, as all had been arranged for a duel on horseback, and this looked like a way of retreat for the Spaniard. Ill as he was Bayard showed no hesitation, and with the courage of a lion declared that he was willing to avenge his honour in any guise. The arms chosen were a sharp-pointed sword or rapier and a poignard, while the armour used included a throat-piece (gorgerin) and a secrete.[4]

When the camp was duly prepared and the champions in face of each other, Bayard knelt down and made his prayer to God, then he bent to kiss the earth, and rising, made the sign of the cross before he advanced to meet his enemy. Don Alonzo addressed him in these words: "Lord of Bayard, what do you seek from me?" And

---

4   Secrete, a kind of steel skull-cap, often worn under the helmet.

he replied: "I wish to defend my honour." Then began the mortal combat between these two valiant men-at-arms, and never was seen more splendid skill and courage. The rapier of the Good Knight slightly wounded the face of Don Alonzo, who carefully guarded this most vulnerable part, but his foe waited until he raised his arm for the next attack, and then aimed at his neck, and notwithstanding the tempered steel of his armour, Bayard's onslaught was so tremendous that the throat-piece (gorgerin) was pierced and the rapier, having no sharp edges (it was only used for thrusting) was driven in so far that it could not be withdrawn. Don Alonzo, feeling himself wounded unto death, dropped his sword and seized the Good Knight in his arms, the two wrestling fiercely until they both fell on the ground.

The terrible struggle lasted for some time, until Bayard struck his foe on the visor with his poignard and cried: "Don Alonzo, recognise your fault and cry for mercy to God...." But the Spanish knight made no reply, for he was already dead.

Then his second, Don Diego, said: "Seigneur Bayard, he is dead, you have conquered;" which was proved, for they took off his visor and he breathed no more. This was a sad trouble to the victor, for he would have given all he had in the world to have vanquished him alive. Then the Good Knight knelt down and thanked God humbly for his success. Afterwards he turned to the dead knight's second and asked: "My lord Don Diego, have I done enough?"

"Too much, indeed, my lord Bayard, for the honour of Spain," was the pitiful reply. Then the Good Knight gave leave that honourable burial should be accorded to Don Alonzo, and his friends bore away the body of their champion with sad lamentation. But we may imagine the joy and triumph with which the noble company present and the French men-at-arms accompanied their hero back to the castle of Monervine.

This duel and the passages-of-arms before with Don Alonzo spread the fame of Bayard throughout all Europe; indeed, his wonderful renown as the flower of all chivalry really dates from this time. You may imagine how bitter the Spaniards were and how they sought for revenge.

After the battle of Cerignola, fought on April 28, 1503, Gonzalvo, the Great Captain, entered Naples in triumph. When this disastrous news reached France, Louis XII. hastened to send a fresh army, commanded by la Tremouille, to reinforce the troops already in Apulia and Calabria. The French general fell ill, and his authority passed into the hands of the Marquis of Mantua, who found himself opposed and beaten back at every point by the genius of Gonzalvo.

At length the two armies came to a stand on either side of the River Garigliano, one of the broadest rivers of Southern Italy, falling into the Gulf of Gaeta. The French had possession of the right bank of the river, close to the rising ground, and had therefore a more favourable position than the marshy swamp on the lower side, in which the Spanish forces remained encamped for fifty days. It was a fearful time, in the dead of winter, with excessive rains, and the soldiers in both camps were driven to the last verge of endurance, while numbers sickened and died. Under these depressing circumstances the bright, cheerful spirit of Bayard, the Good Knight, was invaluable, and his mere presence kept his company in hope and courage. He never missed an opportunity of engaging in any feat of arms, and his famous defence of the bridge is perhaps the best known of all his exploits.

There was a bridge across the Garigliano which was in the hands of the French, and one day a certain Don Pedro de Pas, a Spanish captain, small and dwarfish in body but great in soul, conceived a plan for obtaining possession of it. With about a hundred horsemen he set off to cross the river by a ford which he knew of, and behind each horseman he had placed a foot-soldier, armed with an "arquebuse." Don Pedro did this in order to raise an alarm in the French camp, so that the whole army might rush to defend it, and leave unprotected the bridge, which would then be seized by the Spaniards. Bayard, who always chose the post of danger, was encamped close to the bridge, and with him was a brave gentleman, named le Basco. When they heard the noise they armed themselves at once, and mounted their horses in haste to rush to the fray. But as the Good Knight happened to look across the river he caught sight of about two hundred Spanish horsemen riding straight towards the bridge, which they would certainly have taken without much resistance, and this would have meant the total destruction of the French army.

Then the Good Knight cried to his companion, "My lord the Equerry, my friend, go instantly and fetch our men to guard this bridge, or we are all lost; meantime I will do my best to amuse them until you come, but make all haste." This he did, and the Good Knight, lance in rest, galloped across the bridge to the other end, where the Spaniards were on the point of passing. But, like a lion in his rage, Bayard rushed at them with so furious an onset that two or three of the foremost men were driven back and hurled into the water, from whence they rose no more, for the river was wide and deep. For a moment they were driven back, but seeing there was only one knight they attacked him so furiously that it was a marvel he could resist them. But he came to a stand against the barrier of the bridge that they might not get behind him, and made so desperate a fight with his sword, raining blows on all who came near, that he seemed to the Spaniards more a demon than a man.

In vain they cast pikes, lances, and other arms against him; the Good Knight seemed to bear a charmed life. In fact, so well and so long did he defend himself that his foes began to feel a superstitious dread of this invincible champion when, after the space of full half an hour, his friend, le Basco, arrived with a hundred men-at-arms.

The historian Champier adds that when Bayard saw help approaching he cried, with a loud voice, "Haste ye, noble Frenchmen, and come to my help." Not satisfied with driving back the Spaniards from the bridge, the gallant little company pursued them for a good mile, and would have done more but they saw in the distance a great company of seven or eight hundred Spanish horsemen.

With all his dauntless courage, Bayard had the instinct of a good general, and he said to his companions: "Gentlemen, we have done enough to-day in saving the bridge; let us now retire in as close order as possible." His advice was taken, and they began to retreat at a good pace, the Good Knight always remaining the last and bearing all the brunt of the rear attack. This became more difficult every minute, as his horse, on which he had fought all that day, was so worn out that it could scarcely stand.

All of a sudden there was a great rush of the enemy, sweeping like a flood over the French men-at-arms, so that many were thrown to the ground. The horse of the Good Knight was driven back against a ditch, where he was surrounded by twenty or thirty horsemen, who cried: "Surrender, surrender, my lord!" Still fighting to the last, he could only make answer: "Gentlemen, I must indeed yield to you, for, being alone, I can no longer fight against your might."

If all the accounts of contemporary historians did not agree on the subject we could hardly believe that one hero could keep back two hundred men at the narrow entrance of the bridge for close upon half an hour. That after so tremendous a fight Bayard could pursue the enemy, and defend the rear of his retiring companions, is indeed a marvellous achievement. The wonder is not that he was taken prisoner at last, but that he should have held out so long.

Meantime all his companions had ridden straight to their bridge, believing that the Good Knight was amongst them, but of a sudden a certain gentleman from Dauphine exclaimed: "We have lost all, my friends! The Captain Bayard is dead or taken, for he is not in our company. I vow to God that if I am to go alone I will return and seek him...." On hearing this the whole troop turned their horses and set off at full gallop after the Spaniards, who were bearing away with them the flower of all chivalry. But they did not know it, for Bayard was aware that if they heard his name he should never escape alive, and to all their inquiries he only made answer that he was a gentleman. They had not even taken the trouble to disarm him.

Of a sudden he heard his companions arrive in pursuit, shouting: "France! France! Turn, turn, ye Spaniards; not thus shall you carry away the flower of chivalry." Taken by surprise, the enemy received the French charge with some disorder, and as men and horses gave way, the Good Knight saw his opportunity, and without putting his foot in the stirrup, sprang upon a fine horse whose rider was thrown, and as soon as he was mounted, cried: "France! France! Bayard! Bayard! whom you have let go!" When the Spaniards heard the name and saw what a mistake they had made to leave him his arms (without requiring his parole, which he would certainly have kept), they lost heart and turned back towards their camp, while the French, overjoyed at having recovered their "Good Knight without Fear and without Reproach"--their one ideal of chivalry and honour--galloped home over the famous bridge. We do not wonder that for many days after they could talk of nothing but this thrilling adventure and the gallant exploits of Bayard.

CHAPTER V

The wars of Italy had a wonderful fascination for Louis XII., and he eagerly united with the Emperor, the King of Spain, and the Pope in the League of Cambray against Venice, hated for her great wealth and success.

In the spring of 1509 the King collected another army, in which he made a great point of the foot-soldiers, whose importance he fully appreciated, and for the first time he chose captains of high renown to command them. He sent for Bayard and said to him: "You know that I am crossing the mountains to fight the Venetians, who have taken Cremona from me, and other places. I am giving you the command of a company of men-at-arms ... but that can be led by your lieutenant, Captain Pierre du Pont, while I wish you to take charge of a number of foot-soldiers."

"Sire," replied the Good Knight, "I will do what you wish; but how many foot-soldiers do you propose to give me?"

"One thousand," said the King; "no man has more."

But Bayard suggested that five hundred of these soldiers, carefully chosen, would be quite enough for one man to command if he did his duty thoroughly, and to this the King agreed, bidding the Good Knight bring them to join his army in the duchy of Milan.

The important city of Padua, which had been restored to the Emperor Maximilian, was left through his carelessness with a small garrison of only 800 "landsknechte" (German foot-soldiers). Two Venetian captains contrived an ingenious stratagem for recovering the city. It was the month of July by this time, and immense waggons of hay, from the second mowing, were entering Padua every day. A number of Venetians made an ambush under some thick trees about a bow-shot from the walls, then they hid behind the hay-waggons and crept in through the gates, which at a given signal they opened to their comrades. The German soldiers, taken by surprise, were put to death, and the command was given to the brave General Pitigliano, who repaired and strengthened the fortifications, knowing of what immense importance this city was to his Republic.

Maximilian was extremely annoyed by the loss of Padua, and collected a great army, composed of men from all the allies, to besiege it. He also brought to bear against it the strongest artillery ever used--one hundred and six pieces of cannon and six immense mortars, "so heavy that they could not be raised on gun-carriages, they could only be loaded with stones, and were fired off not more than four times a day." The city was strongly fortified and defended, and it was decided to attack the most important gate which led to Vicenza. This being a most perilous enterprise, the command was given to Bayard of the attacking party. The gate was approached by a long, straight road between deep ditches, and there were four great barriers at two hundred steps from each other, all thoroughly defended. There was a fierce contest at every one of these barriers, and many gallant knights fell in the attack, but the last one was the worst, for it was only a stone's-throw from the battlements. The besieged rained stones on them with their artillery, and the assault lasted more than an hour with pike and battle-axe.

Then the Good Knight, seeing that this became tedious, cried to his companions: "Gentlemen, these men give us too much play; let us charge on foot and gain this barrier." Thirty or forty men-at-arms sprang from their horses and with raised visors dashed at the barrier with their lances, but the Venetians met them again and again with fresh relays of men. Then Bayard shouted: "At this rate, gentlemen, they will keep us here for six years; we must give them a desperate assault and let each man do as I do!" This they promised, and the trumpet was sounded, when with one tremendous rush they drove back the defenders by the length of a lance, and with a ringing war-cry Bayard sprang over the barrier followed by his friends. When the French saw the danger in which these gallant men were, there was such a charge against the final barrier that the enemy was driven back in disorder into the town. Thus the approaches were gained, and the Emperor's artillery was brought forward, and remained there for six weeks until the siege was raised.

A few days later the Good Knight heard, through one of his spies, that in the castle of Bassano, about thirty miles off, there was a strong company of cross-bow-men and horsemen, who made a point of sallying out from the castle and seizing all the supplies of cattle which were on the way to the camp. They were said to have four or five hundred oxen and cows already within their walls. Bayard felt that this must be put a stop to, and his picked companions readily joined him, for this fighting was their very life and they asked for nothing better. So they set forth an hour before daybreak and rode steadily towards Bassano, till they reached a place where the spy pointed out to them a little wooden bridge which the band from Treviso would have to cross, where two men could keep five hundred in check. This the Good Knight left to be defended by a few men-at-arms and archers, who were to remain in ambush until they had seen the troop from Treviso go by, and await their return. Then Bayard gave directions to one of his company to take thirty archers with him, and when he saw the enemy well on their way he was to advance as though to skirmish with them, then suddenly pretend to be frightened and ride off at full gallop in the direction where the main French force was hidden behind rising ground. This was all carried out, and the Good Knight with his men rushed forth upon the pursuers, taking many prisoners, while the rest escaped in the direction of Treviso, but were stopped at that wooden bridge and compelled to fight or yield.

When the fighting was over, Bayard said: "Gentlemen, we really must take that castle with all the spoils in it." When it was pointed out to him that it was very strong and they had no artillery, he remarked that he knew a way by which they might possess it in a quarter of an hour. So he sent for the two captains who were taken and said to them: "I insist that the castle be surrendered to me at once, for I know that you have the power to command it, otherwise you will lose your heads." They saw that he was in earnest, and one, who was the seneschal, sent orders to his nephew and the gates were opened.

The Good Knight took possession of the castle, and within the walls of Treviso found more than five hundred head of cattle and much other booty, which was all sold later at Vicenza and divided amongst the victors. As Bayard sat at table with the two Venetian captains, a young page of his, named Boutieres, came in to show a prisoner he had taken during the fighting--a big man twice his size. The boy had seen this standard-bearer trying to escape, had made a rush at him with his lance, struck him to the ground, and called upon him to surrender. He had given up his sword, to Boutieres' great delight, and the lad of sixteen, with the standard he had taken and his sturdy-looking prisoner, had caused great amusement in the French company. When he was thus brought into the dining-hall before his own captains, the standard-bearer looked very much ashamed of himself, and protested that he had simply yielded to the force of numbers, not to that boy. Thereupon Boutieres offered to give the man back his horse and his arms and to fight him in single combat. If the standard-bearer won he should go free without ransom; but if the young page won the man should die. The Good Knight was delighted at this brave offer, but the Venetian was afraid to accept it, and all the honour remained with the boy, who was known to come of a brave race and proved himself worthy in the days to come.

Most of the French army retired into the duchy of Milan, but Bayard appears to have remained behind with the garrison of Verona. By one of those rapid changes so common in Italian politics, before the end of the year Louis XII. found himself deserted by most of the allies, the Pope, the King of Spain, Henry VIII., and the Swiss having joined the "Holy League" to drive the French out of Italy.

CHAPTER VI

While Bayard was with the garrison at Verona, in command of three or four hundred men-at-arms who had been lent to the Emperor by the King of France, he had some stirring adventures. It was winter time, and that year, 1509, was long remembered for its severity. The soldiers in the town were obliged to send for their horses' forage sometimes to a great distance, and they were constantly losing both horses and varlets, who were waylaid by the enemy, so that a large escort was necessary, for not a day passed without some encounter.

Now there was a village called San Bonifacio about fifteen miles from Verona, where a certain Venetian captain, named Giovanni Paolo Manfroni, was stationed with a number of men, and he amused himself by chasing the foraging parties up to the very gates of Verona. The Good Knight at last became very angry at this bold defiance, and he resolved to put an end to these raids by going out with the escort himself the next time that hay was fetched from the farms round. He kept his plans as secret as possible, but Manfroni had a spy in the city who managed to let him know what was on foot, and he resolved to take so strong a force that he would make sure of capturing the famous Bayard.

One Thursday morning the foragers set forth from Verona as usual, and in their train were thirty or forty men-at-arms and archers under the command of the captain, Pierre du Pont, a very wise and capable young man. The party soon left the highroad to look out for the farms where they were to receive the usual loads of hay. Meantime, the Good Knight, not suspecting that his plan was betrayed, had taken a hundred men-at-arms and gone to a little village called San Martino about six miles from Verona. From thence he sent out some scouts, who were not long in returning with the news that the enemy was in sight, about five hundred horsemen, who were marching straight after the foragers. The Good Knight was delighted to hear it, and at once set out to follow them with his company.

But Manfroni, who had heard of the whole manoeuvre from his spy, had prepared an ambush in a deserted palace near, where he had about six hundred pikemen and arquebusiers. These men were not to stir until they saw him and his party in retreat, pretending to flee from the French pursuit; then they were at once to follow and so completely enclose and defeat Bayard's company.

The Good Knight had not gone two miles through the fields when he overtook the Venetians and marched straight towards them, shouting, "Empire and France!" They made some show of resistance, but soon began to retreat along the lane towards their ambush, where they halted just beyond it, crying "Marco! Marco!" and began to make a valiant defence. On hearing the familiar cry of Venice, the foot-soldiers gave a tremendous shout and rushed furiously upon the French, shooting with their arquebuses, a shot from which struck Bayard's horse between the legs and killed him. Seeing their dear master on the ground, his men-at-arms, who would all have died for him, made a mighty charge, and a gentleman of Dauphine, named Grammont, sprang from his horse and fought side by side with Bayard. But the two were of no avail against the Venetians, who took them prisoners and were about to disarm them.

Captain Pierre du Pont, who was with the forage party, heard the noise and instantly galloped up, finding his captain and Grammont in evil case; for already they were being drawn out of the crowd to be taken to a place of safety. He was only just in time, but he struck out at the captors like a lion, and the men, taken by surprise, let their prisoners escape, and retreated to their troop, which was having a furious fight with the French. The Good Knight and Grammont were soon on horseback again, and hastened back to the relief of their men, who were now attacked front and back, with four to one against them, and the arquebusiers were doing them a lot of damage. Then the Good Knight said to his nephew, Captain Pierre du Pont: "My friend, we are lost if we do not gain the highroad, but if we are once there, we will retire in spite of them, and shall be saved, with the help of God."

"I agree with you," replied his nephew. Then they began to retreat steadily, step by step, towards the highroad, fighting all the way, and they reached it at last, though not without much trouble, while the enemy lost both foot-soldiers and horsemen. When the French at length reached the highroad which led to Verona, they closed in together, and began to retire very gently, turning upon the foe with a gallant attack every two hundred feet.

But all the time they had those arquebusiers at their heels constantly firing upon them, so that at the last charge once more the Good Knight had his horse killed under him. Before it fell he sprang to the ground and defended himself in a wonderful way with his sword; but he was soon surrounded and would have been killed, but at that moment his standard-bearer, du Fay, with his archers, made so desperate a charge that he rescued his captain from the very midst of the Venetians, set him upon another horse, and then closed in with the others.

The night was drawing near, and the Good Knight commanded that there should be no more charging, as they had done enough for their honour, and the gallant little party found a safe refuge in the village of San Martino, in the midst of cypresses, whence they had started in the morning. This was about four miles from Verona, and the Venetian captain felt that further pursuit would be dangerous as help would probably arrive from Verona. So he caused the retreat to sound, and set out to return to San Bonifacio, but on the way his foot-soldiers, who were quite worn out, having fought for about five hours, begged to be allowed to stay at a village some miles short of San Bonifacio. Manfroni did not much approve of this, but he let them have their way, while he and his horsemen rode on to their usual quarters, feeling much disgusted that they had been galloped about all day with so little to show for it.

That night the French lodged in the village of San Martino, and they feasted joyfully upon such provisions as they could find, feeling very proud of their success, for they had scarcely lost any men in comparison with the enemy. They were still at supper when one of their spies arrived from San Bonifacio, and he was brought before Bayard, who asked what the Venetians were doing. He replied:

"Nothing much; they are in great force inside San Bonifacio, and the rumour goes that they will soon have Verona, for they have a strong party within the city. As I was starting the Captain Manfroni arrived, very hot and angry, and I heard him say that he had been fighting against a lot of devils from hell and not men. As I was coming here I passed through a village which I found quite full of their foot-soldiers, who are spending the night there, and to look at them I should say that they are quite tired out."

Then said the Good Knight: "I warrant that those are their foot-soldiers we fought against to-day, who would not walk any further. If you feel disposed we will go and take them. The moon is bright to-night, let us feed our horses and at about three or four o'clock we will go and wake them."

This suggestion was quite approved of; they all did their best with the horses, and after having set the watch, they all went to rest. But Bayard was too full of his enterprise to take any sleep; so towards three hours after midnight he quietly roused his men and set forth with them on horseback, riding in perfect silence to the village where the Venetian foot-soldiers were staying. He found them, as he had expected, fast asleep "like fat pigs," without any watch as far as he could see. The new-comers began to shout, "Empire! Empire! France! France!" and to this joyous cry the bumpkins awoke, coming one by one out of their shelter to be slain like beasts. Their captain, accompanied by two or three hundred men, threw himself into the market-place and tried to make a stand there; but no time was given him, for he was charged from so many directions that he and all his men were attacked and defeated, so that only three remained alive. These were the captain and two other gentlemen, who were brothers, and afterwards were exchanged for French gentlemen who were in prisons at Venice.

Having accomplished their work, the Good Knight and his company made their way back to Verona, where they were received with great honour. On the other hand, when the Venetians heard of the loss of their men they were furious, and the Doge Andrea Gritti sharply blamed Manfroni for leaving them behind.

We may mention here that this Giovanni Paolo Manfroni was a splendid soldier and one of the finest captains of men-at-arms in Italy at this period.

Manfroni had a certain spy, who often went backwards and forwards between Venona and San Bonifacio, and who served both him and the Good Knight; but those treacherous spies always serve one better than the other, and this one hoped for the most gain from the Venetian.

So one day Manfroni said to him: "You must go to Verona and let Captain Bayard know that the Council of Venice wish me to be sent in command of Lignano, a fortified town on the Adige, as the present governor is ordered to the Levant with a number of galleys. Tell Bayard that you know for certain that I start to-morrow at dawn with three hundred light horsemen, and that I shall have no foot-soldiers with me. I am sure that he will never let me pass without a skirmish, and if he comes I trust he will be killed or taken, for I shall have an ambush at Isola della Scale (about fifteen miles south of Verona) of two hundred men-at-arms and two thousand foot-soldiers. If you manage for him to meet me there I promise on my faith to give you two thousand ducats of gold."

This precious scoundrel readily promised that he would not fail to do so. He went off straight to Verona, and to the lodging of the Good Knight, where he was admitted at once, for all the people there believed him to be entirely in the service of their master. They brought him in as soon as Bayard had finished supper, and he was warmly welcomed. "Well, Vizentin, I am glad to see you. You do not come without some reason; tell me, what news have you?"

"My lord, I have very good news, thank God!" was the reply. The Good Knight at once rose from table and drew the spy on one side, to learn what was going on, who repeated the lesson he had learned. Bayard was delighted at the prospect before him, and gave orders that Vizentin was to be well feasted. Then he called together the Captain Pierre du Pont, La Varenne, his flag-bearer du Fay, and a certain Burgundian captain of "landsknechte," Hannotin de Sucker, who had fought with him in most of his Italian wars. He told these friends what he had heard from the spy, and how Manfroni was going to Lignano on the morrow with only three hundred horsemen. Then he added that, if his good companions would join him, these Venetians would not finish their journey without a little fighting, but the matter must be seen to at once.

It was settled that they should start at daybreak and take two hundred men-at-arms. Hannotin de Sucker had his lodging at the other end of the town, and while he was on his way home he chanced to see the spy coming out of the house of a man who was known to be on the Venetian side. The Burgundian captain at once suspected treason; he seized Vizentin by the collar and asked him what he was doing. The man, taken by surprise, changed colour and prevaricated so much that the captain at once took him back to Bayard's lodging. He found his friend just going to bed, but the two sat together over the fire, while the spy was carefully guarded.

Hannotin explained why he felt sure that there was something wrong. Bayard at once sent for the spy, of whom he inquired his reason for going to the house of

Messire Baptiste Voltege, the suspected person. In his fright the spy gave five or six different explanations; but the Good Knight said to him: "Vizentin, tell the truth without hiding anything, and I promise, on the word of a true gentleman, that whatever it may be, even if my death has been conspired for, I will do you no harm. But, on the other hand, if I catch you in a lie, you will be hung to-morrow at break of day."

The spy saw that he was caught, so he knelt down and begged for mercy, which was again positively promised him. Then he told the whole story from beginning to end of the proposed treachery; how Manfroni would have an ambush of two hundred men-at-arms and two thousand foot-soldiers to make sure of Bayard's destruction. The spy owned that he had been to the house of Baptiste to tell him of this enterprise, and to advise him to find means some night to have one of the city gates opened to the Venetians, but he added that Baptiste had refused to do this.

When he had made an end of his confession the Good Knight said to him: "Vizentin, my money has certainly been wasted upon you, for you are a bad and treacherous man ... You have deserved death, but I will keep my promise and you shall be safe with me, but I advise you to keep out of sight, for others may not spare you."

The spy was taken away to be closely guarded, and Bayard said to his friend, the Burgundian captain:

"What shall we do to this Captain Manfroni who thinks to take us by a trick? We must pay him out, and if you do what I ask you we will carry out one of those splendid adventures which were done a hundred years ago." "My lord, you have only to command and you will be obeyed," was the simple reply.

"Then go at once to the lodging of the Prince of Hainault, and with my compliments tell him the whole story. Then you must persuade him to send us to-morrow morning two thousand of his 'landsknechte,' and we will take them with us and leave them somewhere in ambush. If something wonderful does not result you may blame me!"

Hannotin de Sucker started at once and went to the quarters of the Prince, who was asleep in bed. He was roused immediately and soon heard all that his visitor had to tell. This courteous Prince, who loved war better than anything else, was also such a devoted admirer of the Good Knight that he could have refused him nothing. He replied that he only wished he had heard of this sooner, as he would have joined the party himself, but Bayard could dispose of his soldiers as if they were his own. He instantly sent his secretary to four or five of his most trusted captains, who, to make a long story short, were ready at daybreak to meet the men-at-arms who had known of the expedition overnight. They all met at the city gate and set forth from the city towards Isola della Scala, and the Good Knight said to Hannotin: "You and the 'landsknechte' must remain in ambush at Servode (a little village two miles from Isola), and do not be uneasy for I will draw our foes under your very nose, so that you will have plenty of honour to-day if you are a gallant comrade."

All was carried out as arranged, for when the men in ambush were left behind, all the rest of the brave company galloped on to Isola, as if they knew nothing of what awaited them. They were in an open plain, where there was a good view from all sides, and presently they saw the Captain Manfroni riding towards them with his small company of light horsemen. The Good Knight sent forward his standard-bearer, du Fay, with some archers for a little skirmish, while he rode after them at a good pace with the men-at-arms. But he had not gone far when he saw, coming briskly out of the town of Isola, the Venetian foot-soldiers and a troop of men-at-arms. He made a show of being surprised, and bade the trumpeter sound to recall his standard. When du Fay heard this, according to his orders, he began to retire with his company, which closed up round him, and pretended to be going straight back to Verona, but really went slowly towards the village where their "landsknechte" were hiding. An archer had already been sent on to tell Captain Sucker to make ready for the fight.

Meantime the men of Venice, with their combined troops, charged the small company of Frenchmen, making such a noise that thunder would not have been heard, for they felt quite sure that their prey could not escape them. The French kept well together and skirmished so cleverly that they were soon within a bow-shot from Servode, when the "landsknechte" of the Prince of Hainault rushed forth in close ranks from their ambush, and at the word of command from Bayard charged the Venetians, who were astounded. But they were good fighting men and made a bold stand, although many were borne to the ground by the terrible long spears of their enemies. Manfroni made a splendid resistance, but he could do nothing to help his foot-soldiers, who could not escape by flight, as they were too far from any refuge; and he was compelled to see them cut up and destroyed before his eyes. The Venetian captain soon saw that his only chance was to retreat or he must be killed, if not taken prisoner, so he galloped off at full speed towards San Bonifacio. He was followed for some distance, but the Good Knight then caused the retreat to be sounded, and the pursuers returned, but with great spoils of prisoners and horses.

The loss of the Venetians was very great, for none of the foot-soldiers escaped, and there were about sixty prisoners of importance who were taken to Verona, where the successful French, Burgundians, and "landsknechte" were received with the utmost joy by their companions, whose only regret was that they had missed the fray. Thus ended this gallant adventure which brought great honour and praise to the Good Knight. When he returned to his lodging he sent for the spy, to whom he said:

"Vizentin, according to my promise I will set you free. You can go to the Venetian camp and ask the Captain Manfroni if the Captain Bayard is as clever in war as he is. Say that if he wants to take me he will find me in the fields."

He sent two of his archers to conduct the spy out of the town, and the man went at once to San Bonifacio, where Manfroni had him taken and hung as a traitor, without listening to any excuse.

CHAPTER VII

When war began again in Italy at the close of the year 1510, Louis XII. found that he had no allies except the Duke of Ferrara and some Swiss mercenaries. Pope Julius II. had joined forces with the Venetians in his eager desire to drive the French out of Italy, and he was also extremely wroth with Alfonso, Duke of Ferrara. He sent word to the widowed Countess of Mirandola that she should give up her city into his hands, as he required it for his attack upon Ferrara.

When at length the brave defenders had been compelled to yield their citadel, Pope Julius refused to take possession of the conquered city in the usual way by riding in through the gate; he had a bridge thrown across the frozen moat and climbed in through a breach in the walls. It must have been a gallant sight to look upon, when he politely escorted the angry Countess of Mirandola out of the home she had so bravely defended, while she held her head high and boldly spoke her mind, with pride and assurance as great as his own.

When news of the fall of Mirandola reached the Duke of Ferrara he expected that the next move would be an attack on Ferrara itself. He therefore destroyed the bridge which he had made across the Po, and retreated with all his army to his own strong city. The Castello of Ferrara, in the very heart of the city, standing four-square with its mighty crenellated towers, was one of the most famous fortresses of Italy and was believed to be impregnable; only by famine could it be taken.

The Pope's wisest captains and his nephew, the Duke of Urbino, pointed out that Ferrara was thoroughly fortified, well provided with artillery of the newest make, and was defended by an army of well-tried soldiers, amongst whom was the French company commanded by Bayard. One noted Venetian captain thus gave his opinion: "Holy Father, we must prevent any provisions arriving at Ferrara by the river, and also from Argenta and the country round, which is very rich and fertile. But this we shall scarcely accomplish unless we take La Bastida, a place about twenty-five miles from Ferrara; but if once this fortress is in our hands we can starve out the city in two months, considering what a number of people are within its walls."

Pope Julius saw the point at once and exclaimed: "Certainly, we must have that place; I shall not rest until it is taken."

We may imagine the dismay of the governor of La Bastida when he saw a formidable army arrive, for it happened at the time that he had only a weak garrison. He instantly sent off a messenger to Ferrara, before the castle was surrounded and the artillery set in position, pointing out the extreme peril and the absolute need of immediate help. The trusty man made such haste that he reached Ferrara about noon, having taken hardly six hours on the way. It so chanced that he met Bayard at the city gate, and on the Good Knight asking what news he brought, he replied:

"My lord, I come from La Bastida, which is besieged by seven or eight thousand men, and the commander sends me to tell the Duke that if he does not receive help he will not be able to hold the place until to-morrow night if they try to take it by assault ... for he has only twenty-five men of war within the walls...."

Bayard at once hastened with him to the Duke, whom he met riding in the market-place with the lord of Montboison. They thought at first that a spy had been taken, but soon learnt that he was the bearer of bad news. As the Duke read the letter which the commander had written he turned pale, and when he had finished he shrugged his shoulders and said: "If I lose La Bastida I may as well abandon Ferrara, and I do not see how we can possibly send help within the time mentioned, for he implores assistance before to-morrow morning, and it is impossible."

"Why?" asked the lord of Montboison.

"Because it is five-and-twenty miles from here, and in this bad weather it will be more than that," replied the Duke. "There is a narrow way for about half a mile where the men will have to go one after the other. Besides, there is another thing, for if our enemies knew of a certain passage twenty men could hold it against ten thousand, but I trust they will not discover it."

When the Good Knight saw how distressed the Duke was, he said:

"My lord, when a small matter is at stake we may hesitate; but when we are threatened with utter destruction we must try any means. The enemies are before

La Bastida, and they are quite confident that we shall not dare to leave this city to raise the siege, knowing that the great army of the Pope is so near us. I have thought of a plan which will be easy to carry out, if fortune is with us.

"You have in this town four or five thousand foot-soldiers, well hardened and good soldiers; let us take two thousand of them with eight hundred Swiss under Captain Jacob and send them this night in boats up the river. You are still master of the Po as far as Argenta; they will go and wait for us at the passage you spoke of. If they arrive there first they will take it, and the men-at-arms who are in this town will ride by the road all this night. We shall have good guides and will so manage as to arrive by daybreak and thus join the others; our enemies will have no suspicion of this enterprise. From the passage you spoke of it is three miles or less to La Bastida; before they have time to put themselves in order of battle we will attack them sharply, and my heart tells me that we shall defeat them."

The Duke, delighted, replied with a smile: "Upon my word, Sir Bayard, nothing seems impossible to you! But I believe that if the gentlemen who are here agree with you, we shall indeed win...." No one made any difficulty; on the contrary, the captains of the men-at-arms were so delighted that, as the chronicler says, "they thought they were in Paradise." The boats were all prepared as quietly and secretly as possible, for in the city there were known to be many friends of the Pope.

Fortunately it was the dead of winter, when the nights were long. As soon as it was dark the foot-soldiers embarked in the boats, which were provided with trusty and experienced boatmen. The horsemen, led by the Duke in person, also set forth as soon as the twilight came; they took good guides, and had a safe journey notwithstanding the stormy weather. Thus it happened that half an hour before dawn they arrived at the narrow passage, where all was lonely and quiet, at which they rejoiced greatly. They had not been waiting half an hour before the boats arrived with the foot-soldiers.

The men landed and then marched slowly by a narrow path until they reached a very deep canal between the Po and La Bastida, where they had to cross a little bridge so narrow that they had to go one after the other. This took a whole hour to cross, so that it was now quite daylight, which made the Duke anxious, more especially as, hearing no sound of artillery, he feared the fortress had been taken. But just as he was speaking about it there thundered forth three cannon shots, at which all the company was delighted. They were now only a mile from the enemy, and the Good Knight said:

"Gentlemen, I have always heard it said that he is a fool who makes light of his foes; we are now close to ours, and they are three to one. If they knew of our enterprise it would be very bad for us, as they have artillery and we have none. Besides, I believe that on this occasion all the flower of the Pope's army is before us; we must take them by surprise if possible. I would propose sending du Fay with fifteen or twenty horsemen to sound the alarm on the side from which the enemy came, and Captain Pierre du Pont with a hundred men-at-arms should be within a bow-shot to support him, and we will also send him Captain Jacob with his Swiss. You, my lord," he said to the Duke, "with my lord of Montboison, my companions and myself, we will go straight to the siege, and I will go in front to give the alarm. If du Fay is first in position and they attack him, we will go forward and enclose them; but if our party is first, Captain Pierre du Pont and the Swiss will do so on their side. That will astonish them so much that they will not know what to do, for they will think we are three times as many men as we are, and especially when all our trumpets sound forth at once."

No one had anything better to suggest, for indeed the Good Knight was so great an authority in war that all were glad to follow where he led.

The attack was thus made on both sides, du Fay giving such a tremendous alarm on the outer side of the camp that the enemies hastily began to put on their armour, to mount their horses, and go straight towards where they heard the trumpets. The foot-soldiers set about arranging themselves in battle order, but fortunately this took so long that meantime the assailants of du Fay were attacked and driven back by Pierre du Pont, while the Swiss poured down upon the foot-soldiers, whose number would have overwhelmed them had not the men-at-arms rode down upon the papal infantry from the other side.

The Duke and the French company, with two thousand foot-soldiers, who had arrived under the walls without being observed, now joined in the fray from the other side, to the utter confusion of the enemy, who were completely surrounded and cut to pieces. Some of the horsemen of the papal army made a desperate attempt to rally, but Bayard and another captain called their ensigns and rode straight at them, with the cry of: "France! France! The Duke! the Duke!" and charged them with such vehemence that most of them were brought to the ground. The fighting went on for a good hour, but at last the camp was lost and those escaped who could, but they were not many. This battle cost the Pope about three thousand men, all his artillery and camp furnishing, and was the salvation of the duchy of Ferrara. More than three hundred horses remained in the hands of the conquerors, besides many prisoners of importance.

Indeed, we do not wonder that so much stress is laid upon this victory by the chronicler of Bayard, as it was solely due to his energy and resolution. The battle took place on February 11, 1511.

It was at the siege of Brescia that the fame of Bayard reached its highest point. His splendid courage in volunteering to place himself in the forefront of battle and face the dreaded hand-guns of the arquebusiers is the more striking as he had a special hatred of these new arms which were coming more and more into use. All this gunpowder business was detestable to the great knight, who had been trained in the old school of chivalry, where gentlemen showed their skill in the use of arms, and fought bravely against each other, while a battle was a kind of glorified tournament. "It is a shame," he used to say, "that a man of spirit should be exposed to be killed by a miserable stone or iron ball against which he cannot defend himself."

Bayard always seems to us singularly free from the superstitions of his day, but we cannot forget that an astrologer had foretold his death from one of these new machines of war.

When all preparations had been made for the assault of the city, the Duke of Nemours said to the captains of the army: "My lords, there is one thing that for God's sake we must consider. You know that if this town is taken by assault, it will be ruined and pillaged, and many will be put to death, which seems a great pity. We must try once, before they put it to the touch, whether they will surrender."

This was agreed to, and the next morning a trumpeter was sent forth from the citadel, who marched down to the first rampart of the enemy where the Doge, Messire Andrea Gritti, and his captains came to meet him. The trumpeter asked if he might enter the town, but was told that he might say what he liked to those present who had the authority to answer him. Then he gave his message, saying that if they would give up the city they should all be free to go forth and their lives would be safe, but if it were taken by assault they would probably all be killed.

The answer they gave was to bid him return, for the town belonged to the Republic of Venice, and so would remain, and they would take good care that no Frenchman should ever set foot within.

The trumpeter brought back his answer, and when it was heard, there was no more delay for the men were already in battle order.

"Well, gentlemen, we must all do our best.... Let us march," said Gaston de Foix, Duc de Nemours, "in the name of God and my lord St. Denis." Drums, trumpets, and bugles sounded an alarm. The enemy replied with a burst of artillery, and the attacking party from the citadel began their descent down the hill, where the ground was very slippery, for there had been rain in the night. The general and many other knights took off their broad, plated shoes to gain a firmer hold with the felt slippers worn under the armour, for no one wished to be left behind. At the first rampart there was a fierce conflict, for it was splendidly defended, and while the Good Knight's company cried "Bayard! Bayard! France!" the enemy replied with "Marco! Marco!" making so much noise as to drown the sound of the hand-guns. The Doge, Andrea Gritti, encouraged his followers by saying to them in the Italian tongue: "Hold firm, my friends, the French will soon be tired, and if we can defeat this Bayard, the others will never come on."

But in spite of all his encouragement his men began to give way, and seeing this the Good Knight cried: "Push on, push on, comrades! It is ours; only march forward and we have won." He himself was the first to enter and cross the rampart with about a thousand men following after him, and so with much fighting the first fort was taken with great loss of life to the defenders.

But in the very moment of victory the Good Knight was wounded, receiving the blow of a pike in his thigh, which entered in so deeply that the iron was broken and remained in the wound. He believed himself stricken to death from the pain he suffered, and turning to his friend, the lord of Molart, he said: "Companion, advance with your men, the city is gained; but I can go no further for I am dying." He was losing so much blood that he felt he must either die without confession, or else permit two of his archers to carry him out of the melee and do their best to staunch the wound.

When the news spread that their hero and champion was mortally wounded the whole army, captains and men alike, were all moved to avenge his death, and fought with fierce courage. Nothing could resist them, and at length they entered pell-mell into the city, where the citizens and the women threw great stones and boiling water from the windows upon the invaders, doing more harm than all the soldiers had done. But the men of Venice were utterly defeated, and many thousands remained in their last sleep in the great piazza and the narrow streets where they had been pursued by the enemy. Of that proud army which had held Brescia with bold defiance, such as were not slain were taken prisoners, and among these was the Doge of Venice himself. Then followed an awful time of pillage and every form of cruelty and disorder, as was ever the way in those days when a city was taken by storm. The spoils taken were valued at three millions of crowns, and this in the end proved the ruin of the French power in Italy, for so many of the soldiers, demoralised by plunder, deserted with their ill-gotten gains and went home.

Meantime the wounded Bayard was borne into the city by his two faithful archers and taken to a quiet street from whence the tide of battle had passed on. Here they knocked at the door of a fine house whose master had fled to a monastery, leaving his wife in charge. The good lady opened it at once to receive the wounded soldier, and Bayard, turning to his men, bade them guard the house against all comers, being assured that when they heard his name none would attempt to enter. "And rest assured that what you lose in the matter of spoil I will make good to you," he added. The lady of the house led the way to her guest-chamber, whither the Good Knight was carried, and she threw herself on her knees before him, saying: "Noble lord, I present to you this house and all that is in it, for it is yours by right of war, but I pray you to spare my honour and my life and that of my two young daughters...." She had hidden away the poor girls in an attic under the hay, but Bayard soon set her mind at rest, and gave her his knightly word that her house would be as safe as a sanctuary. Then he asked if she knew of a surgeon, and she went to fetch her own doctor, under the escort of one of the archers. When he arrived he dressed the wound, which was very deep and jagged, but he assured his patient that he was in no danger of death, and would probably be on horseback again in less than a month.

Great was the joy of the Duc de Nemours and of all the French army when this good report reached them, and the general, who remained in Brescia for about a week, paid him a visit every day. He tried to comfort him by the prospect of another battle before long against the Spaniards, and bade him be quick and get well, for they could not do without him. The Good Knight made reply that if there should be a battle he would not miss it for the love he bore to his dear Gaston de Foix and for the King's service; rather he would be carried thither in a litter.

Before leaving, when he had placed the hapless city in some kind of order and government, Gaston sent the Good Knight many presents and five hundred crowns, which he at once gave to his faithful archers. The Duke had, indeed, no choice about his movements, for he received most urgent letters from the King of France, who wanted the Spaniards to be driven out of Lombardy as soon as possible, for France was threatened on every side, by the King of England and by the Swiss.

The Good Knight was compelled to remain in bed for nearly five weeks, to his great annoyance, for he received news from the French camp every day, and there was constant talk of an approaching battle. So he sent for the surgeon who attended him and told him that all this worry was making him much worse, and that he must be allowed to join the camp. Seeing what kind of warrior he had to deal with, the good man replied that the wound was not closed but was healing well, and that there would be no danger in his sitting on horseback, but the wound must be carefully dressed night and morning by his barber. If any one had given Bayard a fortune he would not have been so delighted, and he settled to start in two days' time. On the morning when he was to leave after dinner, the good lady of the house came to speak to him. She knew that by the laws of war she, her daughters, and her husband (who had long since returned from the monastery where he had taken refuge) were all prisoners of this French knight, and all that was in the house belonged to him. But she had found him so kind and courteous that she hoped to gain his favour by a handsome present, and she brought with her one of her servants bearing a steel casket containing 2500 ducats. On entering the Good Knight's chamber she fell on her knees before him, but he would not suffer her to speak a word until she was seated by his side. Then she poured out all her gratitude for his knightly courtesy and protection, and at last offered him the casket, opening it to show what it contained. But Bayard put it aside with a friendly smile, and replied:

"On my word, dear lady, I have never cared for money all my life! No riches could ever be so precious to me as the kindness and devoted care which you have shown to me during my stay with you, and I assure you that so long as I live you will always have a faithful gentleman at your command. I thank you very much for your ducats, but I pray that you will take them back...." However, the lady was so much distressed at his refusal that he at length accepted the casket, but begged her to send her daughters to wish him good-bye. When they came and would have fallen on their knees before him, he would not suffer such humility, but thanked them for all their kindness in cheering him with their lute and spinet and singing during his illness, and begged them to accept the ducats contained in their mother's casket, which he poured out into their aprons whether they would or not. Overcome by his courteous persuasion, the mother thanked him with tears in her eyes: "Thou flower of knighthood to whom none can compare, may the Blessed Saviour reward thee in this world and the next." When the Good Knight's horses were brought round at mid-day, after dinner, the two fair maidens brought him some presents of their own needlework, bracelets made with hair bound with gold and silver threads, and a little embroidered purse, which he gallantly placed in his sleeve, and the bracelets on his arms, with many thanks, to the great delight of the girls. Thus with friendly words and courtly farewells he took his leave, and rode away with a goodly company of friends towards the camp near Ravenna, where he was welcomed with the greatest joy and honour by all the French army.

When Gaston de Foix, Duke of Nemours, arrived at the camp before Ravenna he assembled all the captains together to consider what was to be done, for the French army began to suffer very much on account of the scarcity of provisions, which could only be obtained with great difficulty. They were very short of bread and wine, because the Venetians had cut off the supplies from one side and the Spanish army held all the coast of Romagna.

There was also another reason for haste, which was not yet known to the French leaders. Maximilian had long been uncertain and vacillating in his alliances, but had now definitely decided to join the side of Pope Julius and the King of Spain. As usual there were companies of German and Swiss mercenaries both in the Italian army and also with the French, and these owed some kind of allegiance to the sovereign of their land. Thus it was that the Emperor had sent word to the companies of German "landsknechte" that they were to retire home at once and were not to fight against the Spaniards. Now it so happened that this letter had only been seen by the Captain Jacob, who commanded these mercenaries in the French army, and he, being a great friend of Bayard, privately asked his advice, first telling him that having accepted the pay of the French King he had no intention of thus betraying him in the hour of battle. But he suggested that it would be well to hurry on the impending battle before other letters should come from the Emperor and give the men an excuse for retiring. The Good Knight saw how urgent the matter was and advised him to declare it to the general, the Duc de Nemours.

Duke Gaston, who had now heard of the Emperor's letter, said that they had no choice, and also that his uncle, the King of France, was sending constant messengers to hurry on war operations as he was in sore straits. Bayard was asked to give his opinion, and he modestly replied that he had only just arrived and others might know more, but as far as he could learn, the besieged were promised that a large army from Naples and Rome would come to their help in a few days, certainly before Easter, and this was Maundy Thursday. "And on the other hand," he added, "our men have no provisions and the horses are reduced to eating willow leaves, so that each day's delay makes it worse for us. You see, too, the King our master writes to us every day to hasten our movements, therefore I advise that we give battle. But we must use all caution for we have to do with brave and good fighting men, and we cannot deny the risk and danger. There is one comfort: the Spaniards have been in Romagna for a year, fed like fish in the water till they are fat and full, while our men, having undergone much hardship, have longer breath. Remember that to him who fights longest the camp will remain."

At this every one smiled, for Bayard always had such a bright and pleasant way of putting things that men loved to hear him. His advice was followed and all was made ready for a determined assault on the city next day, which was Good Friday. The captains and their men set forth in gallant mood, as though they went to a wedding, and so fierce was the attack of the artillery that before long a small breach was made in the fortification, but the defenders fought so well that it was not possible to break through and at length the retreat was sounded. This was really a fortunate thing, as if the soldiery had begun pillaging the place the coming battle would certainly have been lost, and the relieving army was now within two miles of Ravenna.

It would be too long to follow the whole story of that fierce and desperate conflict, where both sides fought with the utmost skill and valour. The Spaniards certainly carried out their usual tactics of constantly taking aim at the horses of the French riders, for they have a proverb which says: "When the horse is dead the man-at-arms is lost." Their war-cry was: "Spain! Spain! St. Iago!" to which the other side replied by another furious onslaught to the shouts of "France! France!" And wherever the Good Knight passed, "Bayard! Bayard!" was the clarion note which cheered on his company, ever in the forefront of battle. The French artillery was used with great success, and as for the young general, Gaston de Foix, he led forward his men again and again with splendid success. It was late in the day and already the tide of victory was on the side of the French, when the Good Knight, who was riding in pursuit of the flying enemy, said to the Duke: "Praise be to God, you have won the battle, my lord, and the world will ring with your fame. I pray you to remain here by the bridge and rally your men-at-arms to keep them from pillaging the camp. But do not leave, I entreat, till we return." It would have been well, indeed, if he had remembered this, but some time later, in the tumult and confusion, he saw some Gascons being driven across the canal by a few Spanish fugitives, and with his usual impetuous chivalry, Gaston threw himself to their rescue, without waiting to see who followed him.

He found himself hemmed in between the canal and a deep ditch, attacked by desperate men with pikes; his horse was killed and he fought on foot with only his sword. His companions, who had quickly seen his danger, were trampled down or thrust into the water, and in vain his cousin, de Lautrec, shouted to the Spaniards, "Do not kill him; he is our general, the brother of your Queen" (Germaine de Foix). The gallant young Duke fell covered with wounds, and de Lautrec was left for dead, before their assailants turned and continued their flight to Ravenna. It so chanced that some distance farther the Good Knight met them, and would have attacked them, but they pleaded humbly for their lives, which could make no difference now the battle was won. Bayard let them go, little knowing that they had done to death his dear lord and beloved friend, Gaston de Foix.

The Good Knight wrote to his uncle on April 14, 1512:

"Sir, if our King has gained the battle I vow to you that we poor gentlemen have lost it; for while we were away in pursuit of the enemy ... my lord of Nemours ... was killed and never was there such grief and lamentation as overwhelms our camp, for we seem to have lost everything. If our dear lord had lived to his full age (he was but twenty-four) he would have surpassed all other princes, and his memory would have endured so long as the world shall last.... Sir, yesterday morning the body of my lord (Gaston de Foix, Duc de Nemours) was borne to Milan with the greatest honour we could devise, with two hundred men-at-arms, the many banners taken in this battle carried trailing on the ground before his body, with his own standards triumphantly floating behind him.... We have lost many other great captains, and amongst them my friend Jacob of the German foot-soldiers ... and I assure you that for a hundred years the kingdom of France will not recover from our loss....--Your humble servitor, BAYARD."

The brilliant victory won outside the walls of Ravenna was the last successful engagement of the French army which, threatened on every side, was soon "to melt away like mist flying before the wind." The day after the battle Ravenna was pillaged by the French adventurers and "landsknechte" with the usual unfortunate result, that they forsook their masters and returned home with their booty.

This gallant young prince was indeed a terrible loss both to his friends and to his country. His uncle, Louis XII., is said to have exclaimed, on hearing of the death of the Duke of Nemours: "Would to God that I had lost Italy, and that Gaston and the others who fell at Ravenna were still alive!"

It was difficult to fill his place, but Chabannes la Palisse was chosen to the command of the army, as Lautrec had been grievously wounded and was now at Ferrara, where he ultimately recovered.

The French army was already weary and dispirited when the troops of the Pope and his allies bore down upon them in great numbers; and after several attempts at resistance they were compelled to retire to Pavia, which they hoped to defend. However, they had barely time to fortify the various gates before the enemy was upon them, two days later. By the advice of Bayard, a bridge of boats was made across the river as a way of retreat, for the stone bridge was sure to be guarded by the enemy, and, as we shall see, this proved to be of immense value. By some means, the Swiss managed to enter the town by the citadel and advanced to the market-place, where, on the alarm being sounded, they were met by the foot-soldiers and some men-at-arms, amongst whom were the Captain Louis d'Ars, who was Governor, La Palisse, and the lord of Imbercourt. But, above all, the Good Knight did incredible things, for with about twenty or thirty men-at-arms he held all the Swiss at bay for about two hours in a narrow passage, fighting the whole time with such desperate energy that he had two horses killed under him.

It was now that the bridge of boats came into use, and the artillery was first preparing to cross when Captain Pierre du Pont, Bayard's nephew, who was keeping a watch on the enemy, came to tell the company fighting in the market-place: "Gentlemen, retire at once; for above our bridge a number of Swiss are arriving in little boats, ten at a time, and when they have enough men they will enclose us in this city and we shall all be cut to pieces."

He was so wise and valiant a leader that his words were obeyed, and the French retreated, always fighting, as far as their bridge, hotly pursued, so that there was heavy skirmishing. However, the horsemen passed over safely, while about three hundred foot-soldiers remained behind to guard the entrance of the bridge. But a great misfortune happened, for when the French had just succeeded in taking across the last piece of artillery, a long "culverin"[5] (cannon), named **Madame de Forli**,[6] which had been re-taken from the Spaniards at Ravenna, was so heavy that it sank the first boat, and the poor soldiers, seeing they were lost, escaped as best they could, but many were killed and others drowned.

When the French had crossed the bridge they destroyed it, although they were no longer pursued, but a great misfortune befell Bayard. He was, as usual, in the place of danger, protecting the retreat of his company, when he was wounded by the shot from the town of a small cannon called a "fowler." It struck him between the shoulder and the neck with such force that all the flesh was torn off to the bone, and those who saw the shot thought he was killed. But although he was in agony and knew that he was seriously wounded, he said to his companions: "Gentlemen, it is nothing." They tried to staunch the wound with moss from the trees, and some of his soldiers tore up their shirts for bandages, as there was no surgeon at hand. It was in this unfortunate condition that the Good Knight accompanied the French army on that sad retreat from place to place, until at last they reached Piedmont and crossed the Alps.

Less than three months after the victory of Ravenna the triumphant allies had re-taken Bologna, Parma, and Piacenza without a blow; had encouraged Genoa to assert her independence; and Italy, with the exception of a few citadels, had escaped from French rule.

---

5   Cannon of 5-1/2 inches bore; weight of the shot 17-1/2 lbs.
6   Named after the famous Catarina Sforza, the warlike Lady of Forli.

Bayard, who suffered much from his wound, was carried to Grenoble, where his good uncle the Bishop, who had first started him in his career of arms, received him with the greatest affection. He was warmly welcomed and made much of in his native land, and possibly the excitement, combined with his serious wound, was too much for him, as he fell ill with fever and for more than a fortnight his life was despaired of.

Prayers and supplications were made for him throughout the whole country, especially in all the churches of Grenoble itself, and, as the chronicler remarks, "there must have been some good person whose prayers were heard," for the Good Knight gradually grew better, and before many weeks he was as well and as gay as ever. Never was any one more feasted and entertained than he was during the three months when he remained with his uncle, the Bishop of Grenoble. A very interesting letter has been preserved which this good prelate wrote to the Queen of France at this time. He thanks her for her great kindness in sending her doctor, Maitre Pierre, whose skill has had so much effect in curing his nephew. He also informs Her Majesty that he has spoken to Bayard about the marriage she suggests for him, but with all due gratitude he does not find himself in a position to marry, and has never given the subject a thought....

This is exactly what we might have expected from the good Anne of Brittany. She had such a passion for match-making that she had obtained from the Pope a "portable" altar, which always travelled with her, that she might have a marriage solemnised at any time.

CHAPTER VIII

The next war in which Bayard was engaged was that in which Louis XII. was attacked by the King of Spain in Navarre. Henry VIII. was at the same time preparing to invade the north of France, landing near Calais, and the Swiss were already pouring into Burgundy.

As we may expect, Bayard was not long without being sent on some perilous adventure. He was at the siege of Pampeluna with the deposed King Jean d'Albret of Navarre and the lord of La Palisse, when they told him there was a certain castle about four leagues off which it would be well for him to take, as the garrison was a constant annoyance to the French. The Good Knight at once set off with his own company, that of Captain Bonneval, a certain number of adventurers, and two troops of "landsknechte." When he arrived before the fortress, he sent a trumpeter to proclaim to those within that they must yield it to their rightful sovereign, the King of Navarre, in which case they would save their lives and goods, but if the place had to be taken by assault they would have no mercy.

The Spaniards were valiant men and loyal subjects of the King of Spain, and they made reply that they would not yield the fortress and still less themselves. Upon this Bayard put his artillery in position and made such good use of it that a breach was soon made in the walls, but it was high up and not easy to make use of. The Good Knight then sounded the order to assault and commanded the "landsknechte" to advance. Their interpreter said that it was their rule, when a place was to be taken by assault, that they should have double pay. The Good Knight would have nothing to do with their rules, but he promised that if they took the place they should have what they asked for. But not a single man of them would mount the breach. Thereupon Bayard sounded the retreat, and then made an attack with the artillery as though he wished to enlarge the breach, but he had another plan. He called one of his men-at-arms, by name Little John, and said to him: "My friend, you can do me a good service which will be well rewarded. You see that tower at the corner of the castle; when you hear the assault begin take ladders, and with thirty or forty men scale that tower, which you will find undefended." So it turned out, for all the garrison went to defend the breach, while Little John and his men mounted the tower unseen and cried out, "France! France! Navarre! Navarre!" The defenders, finding themselves assailed on every side, did their best; but the castle was soon taken, and the whole place was pillaged and left in charge of the King of Navarre's men.

In this year, 1513, died Julius II., the great warrior Pope, a constant foe to the French, and he was succeeded by the Cardinal dei Medici, Pope Leo X.

Louis XII., having most reluctantly withdrawn his troops from Italy, now prepared to meet an invasion of Picardy by the English. He sent a large body of troops to the assistance of the lord of Piennes, Governor of Picardy, commanded by the finest captains of the kingdom, and amongst these was Bayard. In the month of June 1513 a large army had landed with Henry VIII. near Calais; a most convenient place for the invasion of France, as it was in possession of the English. A strong force was sent on to besiege the town of Therouanne in Artois, but the King himself remained behind at Calais for some tournaments and festivities. When he set forth, a few weeks later, to join his army he had a very narrow escape of being taken prisoner by Bayard, who met him on the way.

It happened that the English King was accompanied by about 12,000 foot-soldiers, of whom 4000 were landed, but he had no horsemen, while Bayard commanded a detachment of nearly 1200 men-at-arms. The two armies came within a cannon-shot of each other, and Henry VIII., seeing his danger, dismounted from his horse and placed himself in the middle of the "landsknechte." The French were only too eager to charge through the foot-soldiers, and Bayard implored the Governor of Picardy, under whose orders he was, to allow him to lead them on. "My lord, let us charge them!" he exclaimed; "if they give way at the first charge we shall break through, but if they make a strong stand we can always retire, for they are on foot and we on horseback." But the lord of Piennes only replied: "Gentlemen, the King my master has charged me on my life to risk nothing, but only to defend his land; do what you please, but for my part I will never give my consent."

The Good Knight, brought up in strict military discipline, was not one to break the law of obedience, and he yielded with bitter disappointment in his heart. The timid caution of the Governor of Picardy had thus lost him, in all probability, the chance of a splendid adventure, for the capture of King Henry VIII. at the very beginning of the war might have changed the whole history of Europe.

As it was, the King was suffered to pass on his way, but Bayard obtained leave to harass the retreating army, and with his company took possession of a piece of artillery called **Saint John**, for Henry VIII. had twelve of these big cannons, to which he gave the name of "his twelve apostles."

The King of England reached the camp outside Therouanne in safety, and a few days later was joined by the Emperor Maximilian, who was welcomed with much feasting. Their combined forces are said to have amounted to 40,000 men, and they soon began a vigorous bombardment of the city, which was bravely defended with a strong garrison, who did their best with the limited means at their disposal. Therouanne was a strongly-fortified city, but the massive walls, which had formerly been impregnable, could not stand against a long siege with this new artillery.

The besieged city was very short of provisions and the great object of the French was to supply these; indeed Louis XII., who had advanced as far as Amiens, was sending constant orders that this must be done at any risk. At the same time he was very anxious to avoid a general engagement as his army would be no match for the combined English and Burgundian forces. French historians tell us that this was the cause of that disastrous encounter which, to their great annoyance, has been called the "Battle of Spurs." They point out that the troops were not sent to fight, but only to revictual a besieged place, and that the King's orders were that, if attacked, "they were to retreat at a walk, and if they were pressed, go from a walk to a trot, and from a trot to a gallop, for they were to risk nothing."

This was the French plan to send provisions for the beleaguered city, a very difficult enterprise on account of the immense army which surrounded it. It was arranged that the cavalry should make a feigned attack on the side of Guinegaste, in order to draw the enemy in that direction, while eight hundred "stradiots" (light horse, chiefly Albanians in the service of France) were to make a dash on the other side, gallop through the defending force, reach the moat and throw in the bundles of provisions which they carried on the necks of their horses. This we are told the

Albanians actually succeeded in doing, and it seemed as if this bold stroke would be successful, for the besieged, under cover of night, would be able to fetch in the much-needed provisions.

The French men-at-arms, meantime, had advanced to the attack and, after some skirmishing with the English and Imperial troops, were beginning to retreat somewhat carelessly, when they suddenly saw a number of foot-soldiers with artillery appearing on the top of the hill of Guinegaste, preparing to bar their way. Only then did they become fully aware of the imminent danger in which they were, and understood that, by some treachery, their plans had been made known to the enemy, who had thus made all preparations for their destruction.

King Henry VIII. had heard of the plan of relief, and before daybreak had placed ten or twelve thousand English archers and four or five thousand German foot-soldiers on a hillock with eight or ten pieces of artillery, in order that when the French had passed by, his men might descend and surround them, while in front he had ordered all the horsemen, both English and Burgundian, to attack them. When the French soldiers found themselves caught in this ambush, and the retreat was sounded by the trumpeters, they turned back, but were so hotly pursued that the gentle trot soon became a wild gallop and they fled in disorder, notwithstanding the cries of their captains: "Turn, men-at-arms, turn, it is nothing!" The Good Knight's company was hurried along with the others, but again and again he rallied them, until at last he was left with only fourteen or fifteen men-at-arms on a little bridge only wide enough for two horsemen to pass at a time, while the stream was too deep to ford as it was dammed up to turn a mill. Here Bayard came to a stand and cried to his companions: "My friends, we can hold this bridge for an hour, and I will send an archer to tell my lord of La Palisse that we have checked the enemy and this is the place to attack them."

We can picture to ourselves how gallantly he fought, for he loved nothing better than to defend a narrow bridge, but the pursuing army proved too overwhelming, for a company of horsemen went round beyond the mill and attacked the brave little party of defenders from behind. When Bayard saw that their position was desperate, he cried: "Gentlemen, we yield ourselves, for our valour will serve us nothing. Our horses are done up, our friends are three leagues away, and when the English archers arrive they will cut us to pieces." One by one the knights yielded, but Bayard saw a Burgundian gentleman on the bank who, overcome by the great heat of that August day, had taken off his "armet" (helmet) and was too exhausted to think about taking prisoners. The Good Knight rode straight at him, held his sword at the man's throat and cried: "Yield, man-at-arms, or you are dead." Never was man more surprised than this Burgundian, who thought that all the fighting was over, but with the cold steel threatening him there was nothing for him but surrender. "I yield, as I am taken in this way, but who are you?" he asked.

"I am the Captain Bayard and I also yield myself to you," was the reply. "Take my sword, and I pray you let me go with you." So he was taken to the English camp and well treated by the gentleman in his tent; but on the fifth day Bayard said to him: "Sir, I should like to return to my own camp for I grow weary of this." "But we have said nothing about your ransom," exclaimed the other. "My ransom?" said the Good Knight. "But what about yours, for you were my prisoner first? We will fight out the matter, if you like." But the gentleman had heard of Bayard's fame and was by no means anxious to fight, surprised as he was at this new point of view. But he was a courteous gentleman, and offered to abide by the decision of the captains. Meantime the rumour spread that the great Bayard was in the camp, and there was much excitement. The Emperor Maximilian sent for him and feasted him well, expressing great delight at meeting him again. After much pleasant talk he remarked: "In the days when we fought together it seems to me that we were told Bayard never fled." "If I had fled, sire, I should not be here now," he replied.

Presently the King of England arrived and desired that the Good Knight might be presented to him, as he had always wished to make his acquaintance. Then they began to talk about the French defeat, and both Henry and Maximilian made some severe remarks, upon which the Good Knight exclaimed: "Upon my soul! the French men-at-arms were in no wise to blame, for they had express commands from their captains not to fight, because our force was not to be compared with yours, for we had neither foot-soldiers nor artillery. And indeed, high and noble lords, you must know that the nobility of France is famous throughout the world. I do not speak of myself."

"Indeed, my lord of Bayard," said the King of England, "if all were like you I should soon have to raise the siege of this town. But now you are a prisoner." "I do not own to it, sire, and I will appeal to the Emperor and yourself." He then told the whole story in the presence of the gentleman with whom he had the adventure, and who answered for the truth of it. The Emperor and the King looked at each other, and Maximilian spoke first, saying that Bayard was not a prisoner, but rather the other knight; still, all things considered, he thought that they were quits, and that the Good Knight might depart when it seemed well to the King of England. To this suggestion Henry VIII. agreed, but required that Bayard should give his word to remain for six weeks without bearing arms, after which time he could return to his company. Meantime he should be free to visit all the towns of Flanders. For this gracious permission the Good Knight humbly thanked both the princes, and took leave of them after a few days, during which he was treated with great honour. Henry VIII. made secret proposals to Bayard that he should enter into his service, offering him high position and great possessions. But this was labour lost, for, as the chronicler says, "he was a most loyal Frenchman."

Therouanne, whose walls had been constantly bombarded with much destruction, was soon compelled by famine to capitulate. The garrison were to march out freely, with all their arms and armour; but the fortifications were destroyed and the town partly burnt.

CHAPTER IX

The next year, 1514, brought many changes in France. First came the death of the good Queen Anne of Brittany, who was greatly lamented by her husband and mourned by all her people. The next notable event was the marriage of the Princess Claude, her daughter, to the young Duke of Angouleme, who was to succeed to the throne under the name of Francis I.

He had not long to wait for his inheritance as Louis XII., having made an alliance with England, was induced for political reasons to marry the Princess Mary, sister of Henry VIII. The poor King was already in ill-health, and he only survived his wedding three months, dying on New Year's day, 1515. He had a splendid funeral at St. Denis, which was scarcely over before all the great nobles of the realm put off their mourning and hastened in splendid magnificence to Rheims to the coronation of the new King, Francis I., a gay and handsome youth of twenty.

The young King at once set about carrying out the desire of his heart--the conquest of Milan. Charles de Bourbon was made Constable of France, and a great army was collected at Grenoble. But secret news was received that the Swiss were guarding on the other side the only passes which were then thought possible for the crossing of armies. One was the Mont Cenis, where the descent is made by Susa, and the other was by the Mont Genevre. Bourbon, however, heard of a new way by the Col d'Argentiere, and meantime sent several French generals and the Chevalier Bayard to cross the mountains by the Col de Cabre and make a sudden raid upon Prospero Colonna, who with a band of Italian horsemen was awaiting the descent of the French army into Piedmont. The gallant little company rode across the rocky Col, where cavalry had never passed before, descended by Droniez into the plain of Piedmont, crossed the Po at a ford, where they had to swim their horses, inquired at the Castle of Carmagnola and found that Prospero Colonna and his company had left barely a quarter of an hour before.

The captains considered what they should do: some were for advancing, others hesitated, for if Colonna had any suspicion of their plan he would call the Swiss to his help, for there was a large force in the neighbourhood. It was Bayard who settled the question by saying: "Since we have come thus far, my advice is that we continue the pursuit, and if we come across them in the plain, it will be a pity if some of them do not fall into our hands."

All cried that he was quite right, and that they must start as soon as possible, but first it would be well if some one were sent on in advance, in disguise, to find out the exact position of the enemy. This duty was given to the lord of Moretto, who carried out the inquiry very quickly, bringing back word that Colonna and his escort were preparing to dine at Villafranca in full security.

They next settled the order of their match: Humbercourt was to go in front with one hundred archers; a bow-shot behind him Bayard would follow with one hundred men-at-arms, and then Chabannes de la Palisse and d'Aubigny would bring up the rest of their men.

Prospero Colonna had good spies, and he heard from them as he was going to Mass at Villafranca that the French were in the fields in great numbers. He replied that he was quite sure it could only be Bayard and his company, unless the others were able to fly over the mountains. As he was returning from Mass, other spies came up to him with the news: "My lord, I have seen close by more than a thousand French horsemen, and they are coming to find you here." He was a little taken aback, and turned to one of his gentlemen, to whom he said: "Take twenty horsemen and go along the road to Carmagnola for two or three miles, and see if there is anything to alarm us."

All the same he commanded the Marshal of his bands to have the trumpet sounded, and to start for Pignerol, where he would follow when he had eaten a mouthful. Meantime the French were marching forward in haste, and were about a mile and a half from Villafranca, when, coming out of a little wood, they met the scouts sent by the lord Prospero to find them. When these caught sight of the approaching enemy they turned straight round and galloped off as hard as they could go. The lord of Humbercourt and his archers pursued them at full speed, sending word to Bayard to make haste.

The French knights rode at such a pace that they reached the gate of the town at the same time as the Italians, and with their cry of "France! France!" they managed to keep the gate open until the arrival of the Good Knight and the rest of their company, when after some sharp fighting it was strongly held. They also secured the other gate of the town, but two Albanians managed to escape and carry news of the disaster to a company of four thousand Swiss about three miles off.

Prospero Colonna was surprised at dinner, and would have defended himself, but when he saw that defence was hopeless he yielded himself most reluctantly to this Bayard, whom he had vowed "that he would catch like a pigeon in a cage." As he cursed his ill-fortune in having been thus taken by surprise, instead of meeting the French in the open field, the Good Knight with his usual courteous chivalry tried to comfort him, saying: "My lord Prospero, it is the fortune of war! You lose now, and will win next time! As for meeting us in the open field, it would be a great pleasure to us French, for if you knew our men when they are roused to battle you would not find it easy to escape...." The Italian lord replied coldly: "In any case I should have been glad to have the chance of meeting!"

Besides Colonna, several great captains were taken prisoners, and the place was found to be full of rich spoils, gold and silver plate, splendid equipments, and above all in value, six or seven hundred valuable horses. Unfortunately for the French they were not able to carry away all this, for news arrived of the approach of the Swiss troop which had been summoned; indeed they entered Villafranca at one gate as the French rode out with their prisoners on the other side, but there could be no pursuit as the Swiss were all on foot.

The chief military advantage of this wonderful raid was that it kept all these Italian horsemen away from the coming battle at Marignano.

Francis I. was delighted to hear of Bayard's success, and finding that the Swiss were retreating towards Milan he followed in pursuit of them, took Novara on the way, and advanced with his army as far as Marignano.

A terrible melee followed, for as the light failed confusion increased. We hear of a most striking adventure which befell the Good Knight Bayard late in the evening. His horse had been killed under him, and the second which he mounted became so frantic when his master charged the Swiss lances that he broke his bridle and dashed into the midst of the enemy until he became entangled in the vines trained from tree to tree. Bayard kept his presence of mind, and in order to escape instant death, slipped gently from his horse, cast off his helmet and the thigh-pieces of his armour, and then managed to creep on hands and knees along a ditch until he reached his own people. The first man he met was the Duke of Lorraine, who was much surprised to see him on foot, and at once gave him a wonderful horse which had once belonged to the Good Knight himself, and had been left for dead on the field of Ravenna, but was found next day and brought back to Bayard, who cured him. This was a most unexpected piece of good fortune, and he was able to borrow a helmet from another friend and so return to the fight, which continued for a while by moonlight.

We have a vivid account of the weird and strange night which followed, when the trumpets of France sounded the retreat and the Swiss blew their cowhorns, as is their custom, and the two armies, with neither ditch nor hedge between them, awaited the coming day within a stone's-throw of each other. Those who were mounted sat on their horses with only such food or drink as they chanced to have with them ... "and it is the firm belief that no man slept during all those hours." In the King's letter to his mother, Louise of Savoie, he says "that he remained on horseback with his helmet on, until he was compelled to rest for a while on a gun-carriage, under the care of an Italian trumpeter ... when the young King asked for water, it could only be obtained from the ditch close by."

When the morning broke, the battle began again with fresh vigour on both sides; thousands of brave men fell, and the noblest names of France were amongst the slain on that fatal field. In the end the victory remained with the French, and the survivors of the vanquished Swiss retreated in good order, for the King, who never knew when he might need their services, gave orders that they were not to be pursued. When all was over, on the Friday evening, Francis I., who had fought throughout with gallant spirit and valour, requested the honour of knighthood from the noble Bayard. In this the young King showed his just appreciation of his most gallant subject, the very flower of French chivalry, the hero of so many battles.

The French army now continued its victorious march to Milan, which surrendered at once, and the King, after leaving Charles de Bourbon as his Lieutenant-General, went to meet Pope Leo X. at Bologna and soon after returned to his own land. Bayard was left in Milan and did good service when it was attacked later by the Emperor Maximilian.

In 1519 the Emperor Maximilian died, and was succeeded in his dominions by his grandson, Charles V., already King of Spain. It was a great blow to Francis I., who had used every effort to obtain this honour himself; and the rivalry then started continued all his life. As Mezieres was in danger of being attacked, Francis I. immediately issued orders that Bayard should be sent to defend it, as there was no man in his kingdom he would sooner trust for so important an enterprise.

This city was of immense importance at that moment, if it could be held against the might of the Emperor until the French army should be made up to its full strength and reach the frontier, where the Germans had arrived, commanded by two great captains, the Count of Nassau and the famous *condottiere*, Franz von Sickingen.

Bayard most gladly obeyed the King's command and lost no time in making his way to Mezieres with certain young nobles, amongst whom was the young lord Montmorency, and with a goodly company of men-at-arms. When he arrived he found the place in a very poor condition to stand a siege, and he at once set to work with his usual enthusiasm to improve the fortifications. He worked himself as hard as any day labourer to encourage the others, and there was never a man-at-arms or a foot-soldier who did not eagerly follow his example. The Good Knight would say to them: "It shall not be our fault if this place is taken, seeing what a fine company we are. Why, if we had to defend a field with only a four-foot ditch round it, we would fight a whole day before we should be beaten. But, thank God, here we have ditches, walls, and ramparts, and I believe that before the enemy enters many of their men will sleep in those ditches."

In short, such was the magic of his eloquence, that all his men thought they were in the strongest place in the world. This was soon put to the test when it was besieged on two sides, from beyond the River Meuse and from the land. Count Sickingen had about fifteen thousand men, and the other captain, Count Nassau, more than twenty thousand. A herald was sent to Bayard to point out to him that he could not hold Mezieres against their arms, that it would be a pity for so great and famous a knight to be taken by assault, and that they would give him excellent terms. And much more of the same flattering nature.

When the Good Knight had heard all the herald had to say, he asked no man's advice, but replied with a smile: "My friend, I am surprised at these gracious messages from your masters, whom I do not know. Herald, you will return and say to them that as the King has done me the honour to trust me, I hope with God's help to keep this frontier town so long that your captains will be more tired of besieging it than I shall to be besieged...." Then the herald was well feasted and sent away. He bore to the camp the Good Knight's reply, which was by no means pleasant to my lords, and there was present a captain who had seen service under Bayard in Italy. He assured the company that so long as the Good Knight was alive they would never enter into Mezieres; that when cowards fought under him they became brave men, and that all his company would die with him at the breach before the enemy set foot in the town ... and that his mere presence was of more value than two thousand men....

This was not pleasant to hear, and the Emperor's captains made a furious attack with their artillery on the ramparts, which continued during four days. The Good Knight noticed that special damage was done to the walls from the camp of Count Sickingen, and considered by what means he could be induced to go back the other side of the river. So he wrote a letter to the lord Robert de la Marck, who was at Sedan, in which he hinted at a rumour he had heard that the Count might be persuaded to become an ally of the King of France. Bayard added that he desired nothing more, but Sickingen must lose no time, for his camp would soon be hemmed in by the approaching Swiss and by a sortie well timed from the town. This information was to be kept quite private....

The letter was written giving other particulars, and was then given to a peasant with a crown and the order to take it at once to Sedan from the Captain Bayard. The good man set off with it, but, as Bayard had foreseen, he had not gone far before he was taken and gave up the letter to save his life. This message greatly troubled Count Sickingen, who was already suspicious of the other general, and was not slow to imagine that he had been betrayed and left in the post of danger. The more he thought of it the more his rage increased, and at last he gave orders to sound the retreat and cross the river, to the dismay and indignation of Count Nassau, who saw that this was practically raising the siege. Angry messages passed between the two generals, until at length they were on the point of actual fighting.

The Good Knight had been watching all this from the ramparts to his great amusement, and he now thought it time to add to the confusion by a well-aimed attack of artillery, which so added to the nervous alarms of the besiegers that next morning they packed up their tents and camp equipment, and the two Counts went off in different directions, while it was a long time before they became friends again. Thus it was that Bayard kept at bay the overwhelming forces of the enemy for three weeks, until the King of France himself arrived with a great army. We see how it was that enemies of the Good Knight could never get over a kind of supernatural terror both of his splendid valour and his endless resources. King Francis sent for Bayard to his camp, and on his way thither the indomitable captain retook the town of Mouzon. He was received with the greatest honour by the King, who bestowed on him the famous order of St. Michael and the command of a hundred men-at-arms. He also made many promises of future greatness, and both he and his mother, the Queen Louise, praised Bayard to the skies. But, unfortunately, the only results of all this praise were a few empty honours and an immense amount of jealousy and ill-feeling amongst the courtiers. Indeed, we find that after this time Bayard never had any important charge given to him, and never attained the position, which he so richly deserved, of commander in time of war. It is very interesting to notice that the "Loyal Servitor"--that faithful chronicler who followed Bayard through all his campaigns, and probably often wrote at his dictation--never allows us to suspect that the Good Knight felt any bitterness at this neglect. Not one word of complaint is ever heard; he never murmured, he asked for nothing; his only anxiety was to serve his country and his king.

If Bayard was not rewarded with the prizes of his profession he was certainly always chosen when any dangerous or wearisome business was on hand.

The Good Knight was not recalled to Court, and it is supposed that, besides the jealousy which his brilliant deeds had awakened, he was also in disgrace on account of his warm friendship for Charles de Bourbon, who was now being driven to despair and ruin through the hatred of Louise de Savoie.

Bayard having been made lieutenant of the Governor of Dauphine in 1515, it was easy to keep him at a distance from Paris at his post, and with his keen and devoted interest in all matters that concerned his country, these years in a far-off province were a veritable exile. Several of his letters written during this period have been preserved, and we have also a friendly note from the King, written in

December 1523, when he had settled to make another expedition to Italy to recover his former conquests there and to restore his prestige. It is evidently written in answer to an urgent appeal from Bayard to be allowed to join him, and, probably in a moment of impulse, he warmly agrees to employ his bravest captain; but, alas for France! it was not to be in the position of command and responsibility which his splendid talents and courage demanded. It was to be his last expedition, with a hero's death as his only guerdon.

In the beginning of the year 1524 the King of France sent an army into Italy under the command of the lord of Bonnivet, his admiral, who had no qualifications for his high post beyond personal courage. He was a man of narrow views, wilful and obstinate, and from these faults in a commander-in-chief great disasters followed. A strong Imperial party, supported by Charles de Bourbon and Giovanni dei Medici, held the city of Milan, and the French camp was at a little town called Biagrasso, when Bonnivet said to the Good Knight: "My lord Bayard, you must go to Rebec with two hundred men-at-arms and the foot-soldiers of de Lorges, and so find out what is going on in Milan and check the arrival of their provisions." Now the Good Knight never murmured at any command given him, but he saw at once what a wild and foolish scheme this was, and replied: "My lord, the half of our army would scarcely be sufficient to defend that village, placed where it is. I know our enemies, they are brave and vigilant, and you are sending me to certain shame; I pray you therefore, my lord, that you consider the matter well." But the Admiral persisted that it would be all right, for not a mouse could leave Milan without his hearing of it, until, much against his own judgment, Bayard set forth with the men given to him. But he only took two of his own horses, for his mules and the rest of his train he sent to Novara, as though foreseeing the loss of all he had with him.

When he had reached this village of Rebec he considered how he could fortify it; but there was no means of doing so except by putting up a few barriers, for it could be entered on every side. The Good Knight wrote to Bonnivet several times, pointing out what a dangerous place it was and that he must have reinforcements if he was to hold it long, but he received no answer. Meantime the enemy in Milan had learnt through spies that the Good Knight was at Rebec with a small company, and greatly rejoiced, for it was decided to go and surprise him by night. This was exactly what Bayard feared, and he always placed half his men on the watch, and himself remained on the look-out for several nights, until he fell ill and was compelled to remain in his chamber. However, he ordered the captains who were with him to keep a good watch on all sides, and they went, or pretended to do so, until there came on a little rain, which sent them all back except a few archers.

It was this very time which the Spaniards and Italians had chosen for their attack. They marched on through the night, which was very dark, and in order to recognise each other they all wore a white shirt over their armour. When they arrived near the village they were amazed to see no one, and began to fear that the Good Knight had heard of their enterprise and had retired to Biagrasso. A hundred steps farther on they came upon the few poor archers on the watch, who fled, crying, "Alarm! Alarm!" But they were so hotly pursued that the foe was at the barriers as soon as they were.

The Good Knight, who in such danger never slept without his steel gauntlets and thigh-pieces, with his cuirass by his side, was soon armed, and mounted his horse, which was already saddled. Then, with five or six of his own men-at-arms, he rode straight to the barrier, and was joined by de Lorges and some of his foot-soldiers, who made a good fight. The village was already surrounded, and eager search was made for Bayard, who was the sole object of the expedition, and there was much shouting and confusion. When the Good Knight at the barrier heard the drums of the enemy's foot-soldiers, he said to the Captain Lorges: "My friend, if they pass this barrier we are done for. I pray you, retire with your men, keep close together and march straight for Biagrasso, while I remain with the horsemen to protect your rear. We must leave the enemy our baggage, but let us save the men." Lorges at once obeyed, and the retreat was carried out so cleverly that not ten men we're lost. The Emperor's people were still seeking for the Good Knight when he had already reached Biagrasso and spoken his mind to the Admiral. Bayard was quite broken-hearted at the misfortune which had befallen him, although it was certainly not his fault, but there is more chance in war than in anything else.

Still, there was more than chance in these disasters of the French in Italy. They had quite miscalculated the strength of their enemies, amongst whom was now the famous general, Charles de Bourbon, late Constable of France. The young French King, at a time when Spain, England, and Italy were all against him, had most unwisely deprived Bourbon of the whole of his vast estates by means of a legal quibble;

and his greatest subject, driven to desperation by this ungrateful treatment, had passed over to the service of Charles V., and was now in command of the Spanish army. It was he who urged the immediate pursuit of the French when Bonnivet, discouraged by ill success and sickness in his camp, retreated from his strong position at Biagrasso. He made one blunder after another, for now that it was too late he sent a messenger to raise a levy of six thousand Swiss to join him by way of Ivria.

According to his usual gallant custom, as the army retired with forced marches towards the Alps, Bayard took command of the rear-guard, and as the Spaniards followed day by day he bore all the brunt of the constant skirmishing which took place. It was a most perilous office, for the enemy was well provided with artillery, and when the Good Knight made a gallant charge with his company and drove back the men-at-arms, he would be attacked by a shower of stones from the arquebusiers. He seemed to bear a charmed life, though ever in the post of danger, for others were wounded or killed while he escaped unhurt until a certain fatal day when the retreating French army had reached the valley of the Sesia beyond Novara. Here it was that Bonnivet saw his expected troop of Swiss allies on the opposite bank of the river, and at once sent word to them to cross over and join him. But what was his dismay when the Swiss captains replied that the King of France had not paid them or kept his word, and they had come to fetch away their comrades who were in the French army. Worse still, when this became known, all the Swiss mercenaries in his camp rose in open rebellion against Bonnivet, and lost no time in crossing the river, overjoyed to leave a losing cause and go back to their homes with so good an excuse.

The unfortunate French commander was in despair and hoping to hide the catastrophe from the pursuing enemy, he ordered a brisk skirmish, in which he took part with plenty of courage and was severely wounded in the arm. The Good Knight Bayard did prodigies of valour, driving back a whole company of arquebusiers, but in the moment of triumph he was struck by the stone from an arquebus and received mortal injury. Raising the hilt of his sword in the sign of the cross, he cried aloud: "Miserere mei, Deus secundum magnam misericordiam tuam!" He refused to be taken away, saying that he had never turned his back on his enemy, and his faithful steward Jacques Jeffrey and his squire lifted him from his horse and placed him with his back to a tree, still facing the foe with a brave countenance.

We have a most pathetic and touching account of this last scene, in which the Good Knight without Fear and without Reproach died as he had lived, bearing himself with humble devotion towards God and loving care and thought towards all men. His friends would have borne him away, but he implored them to leave him and seek their own safety, for he was in such terrible pain that he could not endure to be moved. He sent his last salutations to the King his master, and to all his companions, and took an affectionate leave of his heart-broken friends, who obeyed his command, all but the one faithful attendant who remained with him to the end. This was his steward, Jacques Jeffrey, and we are told of the poor man's grief and despair, while his master sought to comfort him with brave and noble words. "Jacques, my friend, cease your lament, for it is the will of God to take me away from this world where by His grace I have long dwelt and received more good things and honours than I deserve. The only regret that I have in dying is that I have failed in my duty ... and I pray my Creator in His infinite mercy to have pity on my poor soul...."

Nothing could exceed the consternation and sorrow which spread through the French camp when the news reached them that Bayard was wounded and in mortal agony. The same feeling was shared by his enemies, for to them the name of Bayard represented the most perfect knight in all the world, the pattern of chivalry whom every true man sought to imitate from afar.

In sad procession the captains of Spain and Italy came to do honour and reverence to the dying hero. Amongst them the Marquis of Pescara (the husband of Vittoria Colonna) found noble words to speak the praise and admiration which filled the hearts of all. "Would to God, my gentle lord of Bayard, that I had been wounded nigh unto death if only you were in health again and my prisoner; for then I could have shown you how highly I esteem your splendid prowess and valour ... since I first made acquaintance with arms I have never heard of any knight who even approached you in every virtue of chivalry.... Never was so great a loss for all Christendom.... But since there is no remedy for death, may God in His mercy take your soul to be with Him...." Such were the tender and pitiful regrets from the hostile camp for the cruel loss to all chivalry of the Good Knight without Fear and without Reproach.

They would have tended him with devoted service, but Bayard knew that he was past all human help, and only prayed that he might not be moved in those last hours of agony. A stately tent was spread out above him to protect him from the weather, and he was laid at rest beneath it with the gentlest care. He asked for a priest, to whom he devoutly made his confession, and with touching words of prayer and resignation to the will of his heavenly Father, he gave back his soul to God on April 30, 1524.

With the greatest sorrow and mourning of both armies, his body was carried to the church, where solemn services were held for him during two days, and then Bayard was borne by his own people into Dauphine.

A great company came to meet the funeral procession at the foot of the mountains, and he was borne with solemn state from church to church until Notre Dame of Grenoble was reached, and here all the nobles of Dauphine and the people of the city were gathered to do honour to their beloved hero when the last sad rites were performed. He was mourned and lamented for many a long day as the very flower of chivalry, the Good Knight without Fear and without Reproach.

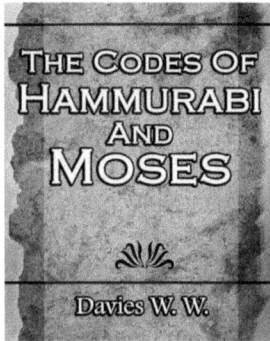

The Codes Of Hammurabi And Moses
W. W. Davies

QTY

The discovery of the Hammurabi Code is one of the greatest achievements of archaeology, and is of paramount interest, not only to the student of the Bible, but also to all those interested in ancient history...

Religion   **ISBN:** *1-59462-338-4*   **Pages:132**
MSRP $12.95

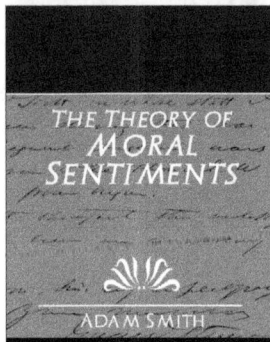

The Theory of Moral Sentiments
Adam Smith

QTY

This work from 1749. contains original theories of conscience amd moral judgment and it is the foundation for systemof morals.

Philosophy **ISBN:** *1-59462-777-0*   **Pages:536**
MSRP $19.95

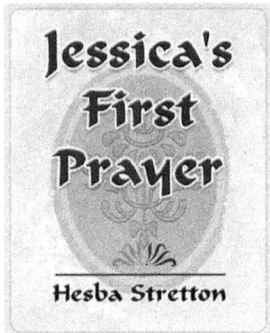

Jessica's First Prayer
Hesba Stretton

QTY

In a screened and secluded corner of one of the many railway-bridges which span the streets of London there could be seen a few years ago, from five o'clock every morning until half past eight, a tidily set-out coffee-stall, consisting of a trestle and board, upon which stood two large tin cans, with a small fire of charcoal burning under each so as to keep the coffee boiling during the early hours of the morning when the work-people were thronging into the city on their way to their daily toil...

Pages:84

Childrens   **ISBN:** *1-59462-373-2*   *MSRP $9.95*

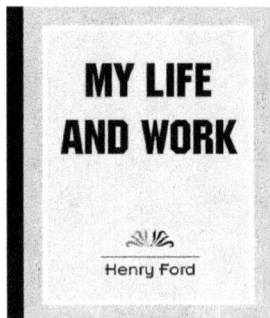

My Life and Work
Henry Ford

QTY

Henry Ford revolutionized the world with his implementation of mass production for the Model T automobile. Gain valuable business insight into his life and work with his own auto-biography... "We have only started on our development of our country we have not as yet, with all our talk of wonderful progress, done more than scratch the surface. The progress has been wonderful enough but..."

Pages:300

Biographies/   **ISBN:** *1-59462-198-5*   *MSRP $21.95*

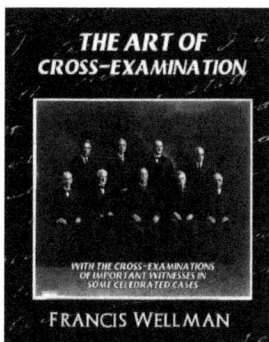

The Art of Cross-Examination
Francis Wellman

QTY

I presume it is the experience of every author, after his first book is published upon an important subject, to be almost overwhelmed with a wealth of ideas and illustrations which could readily have been included in his book, and which to his own mind, at least, seem to make a second edition inevitable. Such certainly was the case with me; and when the first edition had reached its sixth impression in five months, I rejoiced to learn that it seemed to my publishers that the book had met with a sufficiently favorable reception to justify a second and considerably enlarged edition. ..

Pages:412

Reference ISBN: *1-59462-647-2*   *MSRP $19.95*

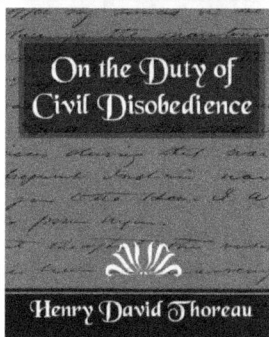

On the Duty of Civil Disobedience
Henry David Thoreau

QTY

Thoreau wrote his famous essay, On the Duty of Civil Disobedience, as a protest against an unjust but popular war and the immoral but popular institution of slave-owning. He did more than write—he declined to pay his taxes, and was hauled off to gaol in consequence. Who can say how much this refusal of his hastened the end of the war and of slavery ?

Law   ISBN: *1-59462-747-9*   **Pages:48**

MSRP $7.45

Dream Psychology Psychoanalysis for Beginners
Sigmund Freud

QTY

Sigmund Freud, born Sigismund Schlomo Freud (May 6, 1856 - September 23, 1939), was a Jewish-Austrian neurologist and psychiatrist who co-founded the psychoanalytic school of psychology. Freud is best known for his theories of the unconscious mind, especially involving the mechanism of repression; his redefinition of sexual desire as mobile and directed towards a wide variety of objects; and his therapeutic techniques, especially his understanding of transference in the therapeutic relationship and the presumed value of dreams as sources of insight into unconscious desires.

Pages:196

Psychology   ISBN: *1-59462-905-6*   *MSRP $15.45*

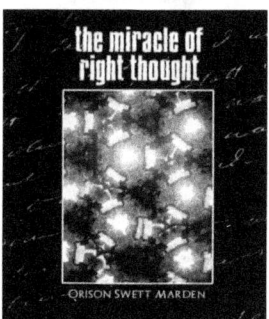

The Miracle of Right Thought
Orison Swett Marden

QTY

Believe with all of your heart that you will do what you were made to do. When the mind has once formed the habit of holding cheerful, happy, prosperous pictures, it will not be easy to form the opposite habit. It does not matter how improbable or how far away this realization may see, or how dark the prospects may be, if we visualize them as best we can, as vividly as possible, hold tenaciously to them and vigorously struggle to attain them, they will gradually become actualized, realized in the life. But a desire, a longing without endeavor, a yearning abandoned or held indifferently will vanish without realization.

Pages:360

Self Help   ISBN: *1-59462-644-8*   *MSRP $25.45*

QTY

The Rosicrucian Cosmo-Conception Mystic Christianity *by Max Heindel*   ISBN: *1-59462-188-8*   **$38.95**
The Rosicrucian Cosmo-conception is not dogmatic, neither does it appeal to any other authority than the reason of the student. It is: not controversial, but is: sent forth in the, hope that it may help to clear...   *New Age/Religion Pages 646*

Abandonment To Divine Providence *by Jean-Pierre de Caussade*   ISBN: *1-59462-228-0*   **$25.95**
"The Rev. Jean Pierre de Caussade was one of the most remarkable spiritual writers of the Society of Jesus in France in the 18th Century. His death took place at Toulouse in 1751. His works have gone through many editions and have been republished...   *Inspirational/Religion Pages 400*

Mental Chemistry *by Charles Haanel*   ISBN: *1-59462-192-6*   **$23.95**
Mental Chemistry allows the change of material conditions by combining and appropriately utilizing the power of the mind. Much like applied chemistry creates something new and unique out of careful combinations of chemicals the mastery of mental chemistry...   *New Age Pages 354*

The Letters of Robert Browning and Elizabeth Barret Barrett 1845-1846 vol II   ISBN: *1-59462-193-4*   **$35.95**
by Robert Browning and Elizabeth Barrett   *Biographies Pages 596*

Gleanings In Genesis (volume I) *by Arthur W. Pink*   ISBN: *1-59462-130-6*   **$27.45**
Appropriately has Genesis been termed "the seed plot of the Bible" for in it we have, in germ form, almost all of the great doctrines which are afterwards fully developed in the books of Scripture which follow...   *Religion/Inspirational Pages 420*

The Master Key *by L. W. de Laurence*   ISBN: *1-59462-001-6*   **$30.95**
In no branch of human knowledge has there been a more lively increase of the spirit of research during the past few years than in the study of Psychology, Concentration and Mental Discipline. The requests for authentic lessons in Thought Control, Mental Discipline and...   New Age/Business Pages 422

The Lesser Key Of Solomon Goetia *by L. W. de Laurence*   ISBN: *1-59462-092-X*   **$9.95**
This translation of the first book of the "Lemegton" which is now for the first time made accessible to students of Talismanic Magic was done, after careful collation and edition, from numerous Ancient Manuscripts in Hebrew, Latin, and French...   *New Age/Occult Pages 92*

Rubaiyat Of Omar Khayyam *by Edward Fitzgerald*   ISBN:*1-59462-332-5*   **$13.95**
Edward Fitzgerald, whom the world has already learned, in spite of his own efforts to remain within the shadow of anonymity, to look upon as one of the rarest poets of the century, was born at Bredfield, in Suffolk, on the 31st of March, 1809. He was the third son of John Purcell...   Music Pages 172

Ancient Law *by Henry Maine*   ISBN: *1-59462-128-4*   **$29.95**
The chief object of the following pages is to indicate some of the earliest ideas of mankind, as they are reflected in Ancient Law, and to point out the relation of those ideas to modern thought.   *Religion/History Pages 452*

Far-Away Stories *by William J. Locke*   ISBN: *1-59462-129-2*   **$19.45**
"Good wine needs no bush, but a collection of mixed vintages does. And this book is just such a collection. Some of the stories I do not want to remain buried for ever in the museum files of dead magazine-numbers an author's not unpardonable vanity..."   *Fiction Pages 272*

Life of David Crockett *by David Crockett*   ISBN: *1-59462-250-7*   **$27.45**
"Colonel David Crockett was one of the most remarkable men of the times in which he lived. Born in humble life, but gifted with a strong will, an indomitable courage, and unremitting perseverance...   *Biographies/New Age Pages 424*

Lip-Reading *by Edward Nitchie*   ISBN: *1-59462-206-X*   **$25.95**
Edward B. Nitchie, founder of the New York School for the Hard of Hearing, now the Nitchie School of Lip-Reading, Inc, wrote "LIP-READING Principles and Practice". The development and perfecting of this meritorious work on lip-reading was an undertaking...   *How-to Pages 400*

A Handbook of Suggestive Therapeutics, Applied Hypnotism, Psychic Science   ISBN: *1-59462-214-0*   **$24.95**
by Henry Munro   *Health/New Age/Health/Self-help Pages 376*

A Doll's House: and Two Other Plays *by Henrik Ibsen*   ISBN: *1-59462-112-8*   **$19.95**
Henrik Ibsen created this classic when in revolutionary 1848 Rome. Introducing some striking concepts in playwriting for the realist genre, this play has been studied the world over.   *Fiction/Classics/Plays 308*

The Light of Asia *by sir Edwin Arnold*   ISBN: *1-59462-204-3*   **$13.95**
In this poetic masterpiece, Edwin Arnold describes the life and teachings of Buddha. The man who was to become known as Buddha to the world was born as Prince Gautama of India but he rejected the worldly riches and abandoned the reigns of power when... Religion/History/Biographies Pages 170

The Complete Works of Guy de Maupassant *by Guy de Maupassant*   ISBN: *1-59462-157-8*   **$16.95**
"For days and days, nights and nights, I had dreamed of that first kiss which was to consecrate our engagement, and I knew not on what spot I should put my lips..."   *Fiction/Classics Pages 240*

The Art of Cross-Examination *by Francis L. Wellman*   ISBN: *1-59462-309-0*   **$26.95**
Written by a renowned trial lawyer, Wellman imparts his experience and uses case studies to explain how to use psychology to extract desired information through questioning.   *How-to/Science Reference Pages 408*

Answered or Unanswered? *by Louisa Vaughan*   ISBN: *1-59462-248-5*   **$10.95**
Miracles of Faith in China   *Religion Pages 112*

The Edinburgh Lectures on Mental Science (1909) *by Thomas*   ISBN: *1-59462-008-3*   **$11.95**
This book contains the substance of a course of lectures recently given by the writer in the Queen Street Hall, Edinburgh. Its purpose is to indicate the Natural Principles governing the relation between Mental Action and Material Conditions...   *New Age/Psychology Pages 148*

Ayesha *by H. Rider Haggard*   ISBN: *1-59462-301-5*   **$24.95**
Verily and indeed it is the unexpected that happens! Probably if there was one person upon the earth from whom the Editor of this, and of a certain previous history, did not expect to hear again...   *Classics Pages 380*

Ayala's Angel *by Anthony Trollope*   ISBN: *1-59462-352-X*   **$29.95**
The two girls were both pretty, but Lucy who was twenty-one who supposed to be simple and comparatively unattractive, whereas Ayala was credited, as her Bombwhat romantic name might show, with poetic charm and a taste for romance. Ayala when her father died was nineteen...   Fiction Pages 484

The American Commonwealth *by James Bryce*   ISBN: *1-59462-286-8*   **$34.45**
An interpretation of American democratic political theory. It examines political mechanics and society from the perspective of Scotsman James Bryce   *Politics Pages 572*

Stories of the Pilgrims *by Margaret P. Pumphrey*   ISBN: *1-59462-116-0*   **$17.95**
This book explores pilgrims religious oppression in England as well as their escape to Holland and eventual crossing to America on the Mayflower, and their early days in New England...   *History Pages 268*

QTY

The Fasting Cure *by Sinclair Upton*   ISBN: *1-59462-222-1* **$13.95**
In the Cosmopolitan Magazine for May, 1910, and in the Contemporary Review (London) for April, 1910, I published an article dealing with my experiences in fasting. I have written a great many magazine articles, but never one which attracted so much attention... New Age/Self Help/Health Pages 164

Hebrew Astrology *by Sepharial*   ISBN: *1-59462-308-2* **$13.45**
In these days of advanced thinking it is a matter of common observation that we have left many of the old landmarks behind and that we are now pressing forward to greater heights and to a wider horizon than that which represented the mind-content of our progenitors... Astrology Pages 144

Thought Vibration or The Law of Attraction in the Thought World   ISBN: *1-59462-127-6* **$12.95**
by William Walker Atkinson   *Psychology/Religion Pages 144*

Optimism *by Helen Keller*   ISBN: *1-59462-108-X* **$15.95**
Helen Keller was blind, deaf, and mute since 19 months old, yet famously learned how to overcome these handicaps, communicate with the world, and spread her lectures promoting optimism. An inspiring read for everyone... Biographies/Inspirational Pages 84

Sara Crewe *by Frances Burnett*   ISBN: *1-59462-360-0* **$9.45**
In the first place, Miss Minchin lived in London. Her home was a large, dull, tall one, in a large, dull square, where all the houses were alike, and all the sparrows were alike, and where all the door-knockers made the same heavy sound... Childrens/Classic Pages 88

The Autobiography of Benjamin Franklin *by Benjamin Franklin*   ISBN: *1-59462-135-7* **$24.95**
The Autobiography of Benjamin Franklin has probably been more extensively read than any other American historical work, and no other book of its kind has had such ups and downs of fortune. Franklin lived for many years in England, where he was agent... Biographies/History Pages 332

Name	
Email	
Telephone	
Address	
City, State ZIP	

☐ **Credit Card**   ☐ **Check / Money Order**

Credit Card Number	
Expiration Date	
Signature	

Please Mail to: Book Jungle
PO Box 2226
Champaign, IL 61825
or Fax to: 630-214-0564

www.ingramcontent.com/pod-product-compliance
Lightning Source LLC
LaVergne TN
LVHW081325060426
835511LV00011B/1856